"Chock full of straightforward wisdom, and delivered with great warmth and humanity, Knupp has a real talent for demystifying complex terms and processes as he covers the waterfront of painful mental health difficulties and their remedies. There's a lot of good self-help here without the usual flashy gimmicks."

—MICHAEL LaSALA, PH.D., LCSW
Associate Professor
Director of the Doctorate of Social Work (DSW) Program
School of Social Work, Rutgers University
Author, *Coming Out, Coming Home: Helping Families Adjust to a Gay or Lesbian Child*

"Knupp has masterfully provided the reader with practical information, theory, and insight in an easy-to-read, concrete, and well-organized guide. Presented in a story-like approach with relevant and well-placed humor, and drawing on his own personal experiences, Knupp's book is filled with helpful jewels of advice. This is a must read for professionals and a practical self-help guide for anyone considering therapy."

—BARRY GLICK, PH.D.
Psychologist
Author, *Cognitive Behavioral Interventions for At-Risk Youth*

"The guidebook we've been patiently waiting for is finally here! It's a delightful presentation of knowledge, wisdom, hope and inspiration. With faith in the human spirit and the ability to heal, the reader is coached through the process of getting help to getting well. Well-grounded in principles of CBT, REBT, and social work, this is a guide that clinicians should assign to all their patients."

—SRINIVAS R. MITTA, MD
Psychiatrist
Capital District Psychiatric Center

"From his extensive counseling experience, pragmatic approach, and many effective years providing treatment, Knupp has produced a worthy guide for anyone interested in learning about the benefits of counseling. It is also useful as a text for a social work course, or as a tool for the therapist. Filled with practical suggestions on important issues that concern the client in therapy, this is a well written, clear, informative, and very practical guide."

—ARLEN WESTBROOK, LMSW, ACSW
Coauthor, *Integrating Delmar 1957: The Story of a Friendship*
Editor, *Writing Women of New England, 1630-1900: An Anthology*

"If you are considering entering therapy, this book is a valuable resource. Written in a very personable style, it includes valuable information to help you on your journey. This is a wonderful guide that I highly recommend!"

—FRED BOREALI, MS, LCSW-R
Clinical Social Worker
Private Practice

"This guide will help most people looking for a path to better mental health. It's for those who want to start therapy and those already in therapy. It's also for their therapists and family members. An easy read, it delivers just what's needed. Knupp has made a successful transition from the spoken word in his own practice to the written word in this handy and practical book. Bravo!"

—KEVIN MCCORMICK, LCSW
Clinical Social Worker
Bethesda House

Be Well!

*A Guide for Entering and
Getting the Most out of Therapy*

Be Well!

*A Guide for Entering and
Getting the Most out of Therapy*

William L. Knupp, LCSW-R, ACSW

OPEN
OCEAN

PUBLISHED BY OPEN OCEAN PRESS

Be Well!
A Guide for Entering and Getting the Most out of Therapy

www.openoceanpress.com

The contents of this publication are for informational purposes only, and not
a substitute for professional medical or mental health advice. The author and
publisher disclaim any liability with regard to the use of such contents. Readers
should consult appropriate professionals on any matter relating to their health and
well-being.

Although this publication acknowledges the contributions of others, the opinions
expressed within those contributions do not necessarily reflect the views of the
author or publisher.

LIBRARY OF CONGRESS CATALOGING-IN-PUBLICATION DATA

Names: Knupp, William L., 1952–, author.
Title: Be well! : a guide for entering and getting the most out of therapy /
William L Knupp.
Description: First edition. | Niskayuna : Open Ocean Press, 2019 |
Summary: A guidebook of recommendations and strategies to help those
considering or receiving counseling and psychotherapy. Includes index and
references. CIP data provided by publisher.
Identifiers: LCCN 2019950978 (print) |
LCCN 2019950978 (eBook) |
ISBN 9781951039004 (paperback : alkaline paper) |
ISBN 9781951039011 (eBook)
Subjects: LCSH: Psychotherapy. | Evidence-based psychotherapy. |
Self-help techniques. | Rational emotive behavior therapy. | Cognitive therapy. |
Psychiatric social work.
Classification: LCC Z6665.7.P79 | DDC 361.06—dc23
LC record available at https://lccn.loc.gov/2019950978

WilliamLKnupp.com

To my wife, Diane.

Acknowledgments

All of the people I want to thank were my teachers, in one way or another. Some are no longer in this world but made it a better place, and others continue to improve it. Some may not know who I am, as I was a quiet but eager student in a classroom lecture or seminar. Others knew me closely, as they were mentors, colleagues, or friends. They all inspired and influenced me, were responsible for my growth as a clinician, and, in turn, the development of this book.

Much gratitude goes to my undergraduate professor at Hunter College, Dr. Herbert Krauss. I am indebted to my professors at the SUNY Albany School of Social Welfare, Drs. Ed Sherman, Max Siporin, and Maureen Didier.

Education during the early part of my career brought me in touch with excellent supervision from the Institute of Rational Emotive Therapy. I want to thank Drs. William Golden, Gary Gilbert, and Ted Wasserman. I especially valued the seminars taught by Dr. Albert Ellis himself.

I had the good fortune to work with many talented and devoted professionals who imparted great knowledge and wisdom. I am beholden to Steve Varden and Bernard Koven, from the Children's Home Society. And for those who supported and pushed me during the many years of challenging work at the Capital District Psychiatric Center. I am forever thankful to John Georgiopoulos, Robert Harvey, Doris Spano, Jack Cadalso, Drs. Srinivas R. Mitta, Michael Dempsey, Kachigere Krishnappa, and Helen Holt.

I also learned a great deal from the many clients with whom I worked over the years. I admired their strength, perseverance, courage, and dignity as they endured their struggles. Their journey to wellness became our journey, and I was honored to be part of it.

I want to thank my longtime friend Neil Ende for helping me come up with the title of this book.

Finally, I want to give a shout out to the editorial staff of Open Ocean Press. Without them this book would be sitting as a draft somewhere in a basement file cabinet.

"I have just three things to teach:
simplicity, patience, compassion.
These are your greatest treasures.
Patient with both friends and enemies,
you accord with the way things are."

—Lao-Tzu
—As cited by Nepo (2000)

Contents

Part I
The Helpers & What They Do

Part II
Thoughts & Beliefs

Part III
The People in Your Life

Part IV
Overcoming Life Challenges

Part V
Other Things to Consider

Introduction

Why write a self-help book when there are already hundreds of them out there? As a therapist, I have suggested self-help reading to clients over the years and found this to be a useful practice. However, I have yet to find a book that can do the job in a clear, succinct, and understandable manner—a book that can hit on all the important points that we go over in my office sessions. I've been looking for that book, one that is easy to read, fun, and gives a good overview of the many ideas I teach when counseling clients. I believe that learning new ideas is at the heart of change. So, I decided to write it myself. This book will serve as a companion guide for therapy and provide support for your journey toward change.

Hopefully, it will help you to become the person you really want to be. I intentionally kept chapters brief for ease of reading and for those of us with a short attention span. As you read, I invite you to take the time to think about the many relevant ideas to process and absorb. Don't be fooled by their brevity, as the chapters are filled with valuable information.

At the end of all my therapy sessions, just as I am escorting my clients out of the office, I usually say to them, "Be well!" In doing this I am expressing my good wishes and sincerity. But I am also giving a subtle directive, one based on the presumption that wellness is possible and in their control. It is determined by their willingness and ability to set reasonable goals and achieve them. My assertion is that *emotional wellness* will come when the person realizes that therapy isn't magic and that real help cannot be given or received without some effort from both sides. Help is certainly given, but it also has to be taken and used for positive outcomes.

Does this mean that you have to work at change? The answer to this question is a resounding "Yes!" I'm sorry to break the news that w-o-r-k is a four-letter word, but it is necessary. I'm sure you've heard your teachers say, "This course material will not be learned by staying passive or through the magic of osmosis." Or maybe you also heard the following: "What you get out of it will be exactly what you put into it." Yes, it is true that therapy involves work, but don't let this overwhelm you. Therapy will proceed at a pace that works for you. Ultimately, it is for your benefit and not designed to defeat you.

So, you decided to start therapy. This is a good decision because it means that you are truly committed to participate in a process of change. What can you expect? Therapy will allow you the opportunity to develop an open, honest and genuine helping relationship with a therapist of your choice. Your therapist will give you emotional support, education, and feedback through reflective comments and interpretations. You'll also be offered suggestions, advice, coaching, and Socratic dialogue to help you think and act in ways that are more productive and rewarding. And your therapist will provide an environment conducive to introspection and insight.

However, your therapist can't do it all for you. Even therapy is a form of self-help. You've certainly heard the age-old adage: "God helps those who help themselves." Whether you believe in a higher power or not, it is most important that you try to believe in yourself! Although you may have to overcome some huge obstacles along the way, you can do this! You have more strength and positive energy than you think.

There are no gimmicks in therapy, though you will learn some new techniques and strategies that will help you along the way. You certainly want to *feel* better and, if at all possible, actually get better. You will pick up some helpful tools during this process, and you'll need to push yourself a bit to use them. Sometimes you'll need to stretch yourself outside of your comfort zone.

As therapy moves forward, you'll be doing various *homework* assignments. These could include referring to charts, creating checklists, filling in forms, journaling, reading new materials, disputing your self-disturbing beliefs, and experimenting with new behaviors. One helpful metaphor for therapy is to think of yourself as a mechanic, carrying around a well-stocked toolbox. Just having the tools sit in your toolbox won't help when the machine starts to break down. You've got to understand the machine with its problems, and then select the right tools for the job. After some experience with this, you'll get better at it; you'll find that your work will pay off. The problems will become more manageable and they just might go away altogether.

Keep in mind that therapy is not only a one-hour session once a week. As I've already said, it is not something done to you as you sit back passively waiting for the results. Rather, it is something done in collaboration with your therapist in a trusting relationship. It is a resource and place to learn about change. Try to take what comes out of each session and learn how to apply it over the course of your day-to-day life. Your therapist will guide you in this process.

As you go forward, recognize that this book is written with an emphasis on *cognitive behavioral therapy* (CBT). Not all therapists subscribe to this model and you may want to consider this when selecting a mental health professional to help you. In this book CBT is considered an umbrella term with its historical roots in the works of Albert Ellis' *rational therapy*, and Aaron T. Beck's *cognitive therapy*. *Rational therapy* was re-named *rational emotive therapy* (RET) and is currently known as *rational emotive behavior therapy* (REBT).

Essentially, CBT is the practice of identifying and correcting *distorted thinking* to improve mental health. As it has evolved in over half a century, CBT practitioners have also developed its focus on emotive and behavioral factors. The ideas in these pages are based on *best practice* standards of today and can likely benefit all readers, no matter what type of helper they are seeing. However, for best results while using this book, a trained CBT therapist is recommended.

Another quality that sets this book apart from others is the fact that it is written by a clinical social worker. This is im-portant because professionals in the field of *social work* look at many aspects impacting the individual and the family. These may include social, cultural, and biological, to name a few. The social worker has the unique advantage of incorporating these aspects into the therapy to work with the *whole person*. When these important concepts are added to CBT, the approach be-comes a powerful formula for success.

If you truly want your life to start heading in a new direc-tion, it will require a strong desire and a concerted effort—a willingness to take a new look at your situation and make the necessary changes. Is it now time for you to get back on track? Is it possible for you to feel more pleasure and satisfaction in your life? If you are answering "Yes" to these questions, then keep reading. Allow yourself to go forward and accept the idea that you truly deserve to be well.

Part I

---

*The Helpers &
What They Do*

1

Go to a Mental Health Professional

A mental health professional is usually a member of one of the three major disciplines: social work, psychology, or psychiatry. Nowadays, you may also find nurse practitioners, psychiatric nurses, and a variety of other counselors (such as those in the fields of addiction or rehabilitation) all providing mental health services. Each may work independently or in a clinical setting as part of a team of professionals, all focused on helping their clients get better.

A *professional* is someone who has completed a recognized course of study in an accredited university with a specialty in one of the mental health disciplines. Such an education requires both academic and clinical experience culminating in a graduate degree that extends beyond the traditional baccalaureate. Upon graduation, tests for national boards and state licensure must be successfully completed before starting an independent practice.

Most professionals are members of their respective discipline organizations. These organizations provide journal publications, educational conferences, specialty certifications, and a code of ethics for all of their members. Professional organizations are involved in the development of quality standards of *best practice*, to ensure that treatment is conducted in an effective and beneficial manner. As a clinical social worker, I am a member of the National Association of Social Workers (NASW).

Most people think of a psychologist when considering mental health counseling. But a psychologist is not the only mental health professional. Keep in mind that you have choices. "Did you know that social workers provide most of the country's mental health services? According to government sources, 60% of mental health professionals are clinically trained social workers" (NASW, 2013).

A *clinical social worker* requires a masters degree from an accredited graduate school. This is a two-year full time program of coursework and practicum field instruction. Although every state has its own licensing requirements, most follow nationally established guidelines. For example in New York State, after graduating, a social worker is eligible to take the licensure exam to become a Licensed Master Social Worker (LMSW). After 3 years of appropriate clinical supervision as an LMSW in an authorized setting, the social worker is then qualified to take the licensure exam to become a Licensed Clinical Social Worker (LCSW). An additional 3 years of supervised practice is required under the New York State Insurance Law for the LCSW to obtain the privilege to perform independent psychotherapy, adding an "R" to the credential. The LCSW-R is the recognized standard for independent practice in New York, with the ability to accept third party payments from health insurance companies.

A *psychologist* is a mental health practitioner with a Ph.D. degree, which is a doctorate of philosophy in the field of psychology. There are also programs offering Psy.D. degrees, which is a professional doctorate in psychology. Both are eligible for state licensure if they meet the specific requirements. It takes anywhere from 4 to 6 years of full-time study to complete a doctoral degree. In addition to coursework and classroom seminars, all programs require practicum field experience along with a one-year full-time pre-doctoral internship. The graduate psychology student participates in active clinical research while also developing skills in psychometrics and psychotherapy. The doctorate is granted after successful completion of qualifying exams, a written comprehensive dissertation, a verbal defense of this dissertation before an expert panel, and an internship. Licensure for a psychologist to practice in New York State requires a Ph.D. or its equivalent, 2 years of full time supervised experience, one of which must be after the doctorate is awarded, and successful completion of a written licensing exam.

A *psychiatrist* is a medical doctor with the ability to treat mental health conditions using psychoactive or psychotropic medications as well as psychotherapy. A psychiatrist may be affiliated with a hospital and have privileges to admit and treat patients within a safe medical setting. Some provide procedures such as electroconvulsive therapy (ECT). Many have private practices, just as other practitioners, where patients are seen in the privacy of an office setting. To become a psychiatrist one must first complete training at an accredited 4-year medical school or school of osteopathic medicine to earn an M.D. or D.O. degree. After medical school, doctors enter a residency program in psychiatry, and they take a three-step national exam for licensure. In New York, after passing the national exam and having at least one year of post-doctoral training, application is made for licensure as a physician. To achieve board certification in psychiatry, a doctor must hold a license to practice medicine, have completed residency training in psychiatry, and have successfully passed specialty written and oral certification examinations.

So, as you can see, all mental health professionals study long and hard to earn the right to work with you. They care about what they do and really want to help you resolve your emotional difficulties.

The helping relationship that develops between you and your therapist involves more than the practitioner simply using his or her expertise to treat you. It involves mutual trust, and this takes some risk on your part. Self-disclosure is necessary for progress to be made. It will take time for your therapist to get to know you and for you to begin to feel comfortable with your therapist.

Your therapist will ask a lot of questions initially as part of taking an extensive psychosocial history. Be prepared for this. Some questions may not have an easy answer. The first few sessions may be the most difficult, but you can get through it!

As therapy proceeds, you will become more familiar and comfortable with sessions, and begin to feel supported and respected by your therapist. More collaborative and targeted work will occur as sessions move forward.

Self-disclosure is an essential part of therapy, and this is why everything you say is protected by professional ethics and legal *confidentiality*. As you probably know, every therapist has a strong professional and legal obligation to protect this confidentiality. There are some rare exceptions, however. For example, when there is child abuse or potential danger to you or others, the therapist is duty-bound to communicate with appropriate authorities and others to protect those who are at risk, including you. Your therapist is a *mandated reporter* of such information to warn and protect others from potential imminent harm. Although few clients experience this level of desperation, it is reassuring to know that help is there and safety is upheld for all involved.

As you move forward with therapy, let me advise you to not place your therapist on too high a pedestal. If you do this, you're likely to get disappointed at some point. Too many people drop out of therapy much too soon for this reason. Your therapist is only human and all humans are fallible. Despite the years of preparation and training, he or she can't really read your mind, and can't predict everything that's going to happen in and out of sessions. Your therapist might even make a mistake now and then. Don't expect perfection because you won't find it anywhere.

A better approach is to give your therapist the benefit of the doubt. Know that he or she really cares and wants to help you. Give yourself a chance to stick it out and don't be afraid to say something when you feel they're not proceeding the way you think they should. This will help to solidify the relationship and make it more meaningful.

Of course, there may be times when the chemistry is just not there and you may experience little, if any, *goodness of fit* with your therapist. You'll know it if this is how you feel. Some personalities just don't match and won't work well together. If that's the case, discuss it openly and decide to make a switch. There is a therapist out there for you!

2

Go Ahead and Enter Therapy

What are the therapies available to you? This is not a secret! Most people have some idea of what to expect. But it's time to throw out the mystery and drama that you have seen in the movies. That's what sells tickets and is usually not the reality.

Individual therapy involves a one-on-one interaction between you and your therapist. The therapist guides the sessions and offers assistance through inquiry and feedback. It is important to discuss feelings because there is value in emotional release. In addition to active listening, interpretive comments and suggestions, various other techniques may be used. These may include role-play rehearsals, problem-solving, imagery, relaxation, journaling, format writings, in vivo assignments, self-monitoring, and many more.

An REBT therapist will help you identify the errors in your thinking, challenge them, and change the way you evaluate situations. You will also be asked to try out alternative positive behaviors. The goal is to move forward in your life by thinking, feeling and acting in a more productive and self-enhancing manner. The REBT therapist is trained to work with clients by creating a supportive atmosphere of empathy, compassion, and unconditional regard. *Respect* is a given with all professionally trained therapists, whether or not they practice REBT.

Family therapy involves all members of the family unit usually seen together. Sometimes the therapist will prefer to see separate parts of the family, such as the parents or the children. The clinical assumptions are as follows: (1) everyone is affected by the disturbance of the identified client, and (2) this disturbance may be a reflection of or exacerbated by other dysfunction within the family system. Focus is on the family structure and process, including faulty communication, boundaries, rules, and culture.

Marital therapy, also called marriage counseling, is usually done in conjoint sessions with both partners present. However, the therapist may sometimes request individual sessions with each partner. Here the relationship is examined, as well as individual perceptions, values, and expectations. Commitment to the marital relationship is essential for a positive prognosis.

Group therapy utilizes group interaction as a therapeutic tool. It can be facilitated by one therapist but is often run by a co-therapist team. Groups are usually comprised of six to ten individuals with similar issues. Group sessions may last longer than the typical one-hour time frame. Groups may be open or closed. An open group allows new members to join at various intervals of the group's life, while a closed group keeps its original participants.

Environmental therapy involves a change in milieu or living environment. Clients learn to improve living skills while focusing on their individual disturbance. They receive help from staff and other clients through re-education efforts and various therapeutic experiences. These settings are often residential, such as hospitals, rehabilitation programs, and halfway houses. Day treatment centers also use this approach.

Social intervention has traditionally been the bailiwick of the social worker, caseworker, or case manager. This type of treatment emphasizes concrete needs and living conditions. Referrals are made to help the client improve in areas such as housing, employment, income subsidies, food, nutrition, clothing, and medical services. Individuals who are struggling with basic needs are often overwhelmed by the bureaucratic red tape required by welfare agencies offering entitlements. Advocacy by a knowledgeable professional may be needed to achieve these goals.

Medication therapy is a form of treatment offered by a licensed medical practitioner. This therapy strives to reduce or eliminate symptoms by prescribing medication designed to assist with brain chemistry and physiology. Medical supervision is needed to monitor the efficacy of the medication and minimize side effects.

You can now see that there are many different modalities or forms of therapy available and the approaches used may depend on the problem, the practice of the mental health professional, and the choice you make about where to go for help. *Goodness of fit* will depend on the style and skills of the therapist you choose and your own personality. Keep in mind that the relationship developed between you and your therapist is a huge factor in your progress.

You may not always feel comfortable in all sessions. Therapy can be difficult because you will be asked to "open up" about your life. Personal and sensitive moments may lead to feeling exposed and vulnerable. It is very important that you feel safe, respected, heard, validated, and confident about the journey you are taking. You need to believe that your therapist understands you, fully considers your best interests, and is genuinely committed to helping you successfully reach your goals.

3

I Am What I Feel— Really?

Not really! You see, language can be misleading. It may lead one to believe that a state of being is forever and defines who you are. For example, if you say, "I am tired," one can take that literally to mean this will always be the case. You are tired and will never be anything else but tired. The same literal meaning is sometimes placed on other feelings. Pick one: sadness, anger, anxiety, or anything else. If you say, "I am sad," then based on this language interpretation, you may end up not only feeling sad today but be doomed to be sad for the rest of your living years. That's quite an ominous proposition!

The same is true with labels used by health professionals or insurance agencies. A *label*, like a *diagnosis*, is used to justify a form of treatment or to communicate in shorthand with other professionals. It does not define *who* you are, and it is not meant to be permanent. It is simply a short cut to describe a current state of being.

Consider the statements, "I am an alcoholic," or "I am a kleptomaniac." Again, taken literally, one may think that this defines who they always will be, and this sense of permanence gives us little hope. Such are the limitations of the language we speak. It is often taken as absolute, and this can interfere with good mental health. Such labels tend to express only part of the reality. That is why good mental health requires a more precise use of language.

What do I mean by a more precise use of language? Well, if one truly is tired, this can be better expressed in terms of the *now*. "I am tired *now*, and expect to be for awhile, until I get some rest." You bet! Go take a nap, because no one wants to be with someone who is tired and cranky. Later, you'll be refreshed, and we can enjoy our time together. We'll go out and have some fun!

But what if you feel something that's more emotionally taxing? Let's take anxiety, for example. When you feel anxious, you may forget that it is a feeling in the now, and like all feelings, it comes at different times and levels of intensity. You might think of yourself as a "nervous wreck," though this would only serve to prolong your misery. Again, I want to stress, that your experience of anxiety is what you feel *right now*, and can best be described as a temporary experience, which will come and go. You can make matters much worse by defining yourself as an "anxious person," rather than a person who struggles now and then with anxiety. The same is true of any other feeling. If you get too angry now and then, does this make you an angry person? I'm willing to take an educated guess that you're not angry 100% of the time. Am I right?

So, you are a person who feels something. That's great! Some people work very hard at not feeling anything. They try to stay numb. They make their lifetime job avoiding one of the very important things that contributes to our humanity. If you don't *feel* anything then you don't get to experience the joys of life. Isn't that what we are all after? Isn't that the whole point of what life is all about? It is truly unfortunate when people are so self-defeating. But, it does speak to how complicated we are as humans.

Yes, we are a complicated bunch because we are not only made up of feelings. We are thinking-doing machines, as well, strongly influenced by past experiences, our physical make-up, and interaction with our environment. Wow! That says a lot.

It all starts at the point of conception and then development in your mother's womb. We are a mix, yes, a blending of our biological parents. This means the genes from both mom and dad are inherited, and this is out of our hands. It is not in our control that we have them. These genes are part of us waiting patiently to come out and be expressed. Some are very apparent and show up in our appearance, like the color of our eyes or hair. Do you look like your parents? Other genes are waiting to show up in your temperament, behavior, and medical profile. This inherited potential sitting in the genes is called your *genotype*.

Your genotype may or may not come out, depending on your environment, your experiences, and what you do. A light bulb in your house won't automatically turn on unless the switch is flicked. The same is true about your genotype, and once this switch is flicked, it is turned on for you and all in the world to see—it then becomes what is called your *phenotype*.

But how does this potential get turned on? Some of it is a natural process, an unfolding of your human development. And some of it is a result of your interaction with the environment. For example, have you ever noticed second or third generation actors, musicians, or athletes? Their potential is inherited and then fostered. It would be wasted if the environment didn't offer opportunities for their learning and growth in the areas where they showed natural talent, interest, and motivation. All of this positive energy is built into their physical being.

So, what does all this mean when it comes to problems in living? Let's take an example from the problem area of addiction. What if your mother used alcohol or crack when pregnant? Not a good idea. The environment in the womb became toxic and you may have started your life on the wrong foot. You may have entered the world already shaking and falling behind others that were better nurtured. What if one or both of your parents had an alcohol problem but were careful during conception and pregnancy? You may have been born looking normal and healthy, but there is a strong possibility that you inherited an alcohol sensitive gene. You too could grow up to find yourself having a drinking problem. You could theoretically switch this gene on by having a beer or two or three or more.

The good news is that you do have some choice and could allow it to sit quietly. It can remain inactive and not cause you any trouble. I know this is hard to swallow, but the creation of your phenotype is more in your hands than you think. If you know that your mom, dad, and grandparents were all problem drinkers, wouldn't it be a good idea for you to just not pick up an alcoholic beverage? Wouldn't it be better to avoid that beer or cocktail? The same holds true for drugs such as crack, cocaine, heroin, methamphetamine, and others. They all have strong addictive qualities and you may have an internal magnet to use and keep using them. Is it worth taking that risk?

To deny yourself something is a hard thing to do. There can be so much working against you. Though you may have picked up some flawed genes by no fault of your own, you may need to also contend with learning from poor role models, or pressure from your family environment, misguided friends, and the wider culture. They may all seem to push you to conform in a way that brings your worst foot forward. If you have a problem with alcohol or drugs, how could you enjoy that next celebration without drinking or getting high? Others will insist that you drink or use drugs with them.

Your experience may be similar with other problems as well. For example, what if you struggle with weight and eating too much? How can you not celebrate that next joyous occasion without a hearty dinner and a nice size piece of cake for dessert? Is there no hope? What is a person to think and do?

What you feel certainly affects your thoughts and actions. For example, if you feel depressed, you may think of yourself as not having desirable traits and think too negatively about yourself to participate in social events. The end result is social isolation. You stop any exposure to what would otherwise be very pleasurable experiences.

An interesting but difficult reverse to this scenario would be to push yourself to attend that social event, despite your negative thoughts. Taking clear positive action would help in working through your negative self-doubting thoughts. This may seem counter-intuitive, but after you give it a try you will find that you did the right thing and feel much better. Just waiting to feel better while feeling sad and disillusioned may only prolong the suffering. Positive action will help you to more clearly come to the realization that it is not good for you to just be what you feel. By following your feelings alone, your decisions are not always based on fact and reality.

So, let's get back to the original premise of this chapter. Is it true that you are only what you feel? Of course it's not true. It's only partly true. As I have already mentioned, there are so many other things to consider. Don't forget that you are a person brought into this world with both good and bad potential. The genetic makeup that was handed down to you and your early life experiences were not in your control. You learned many things as you grew and interacted with the world. A strong wish for approval, a desire for acceptance, and pressure to conform were behind the thoughts and behaviors that often worked well for you. However, at other times, these thoughts and behaviors may have led you into serious trouble. You need to know that you now have the ability to make the right choices. How you think and what you do can empower you! This is part of the secret to feeling better, getting better, and reaching your goals.

As you progress in therapy, keep in mind that you are indeed a complex person—a lot has gone into the making of you. The human clay given to us by the guy or gal upstairs certainly has some limitations. After all, aren't we all fallible? This is what makes us human.

Despite such fallibility, it's important to recognize that this clay can be molded. Think of this: You are the one who can be the great sculptor, and you are the one who can turn yourself into a wonderful work of art. Commitment to therapy can get you there. It's a journey that can make a huge difference in your life.

4

I Have Symptoms— Blindsided

A *symptom* lets you know that something is wrong. The catch is that you may not always know why. When you eat too much, you may get a bellyache. This symptom simply tells you that you put more in your stomach than it can handle. When your car is out of gas, it won't run. If your tire gets punctured, it will deflate. Emotional problems also have symptoms giving the message that your system is not working like its usual self.

The medical community has a model for addressing problems at a time when your body is breaking down and needing help. You learn this model by experience when you are very young and continue to use it throughout your life. If you have a cough that just doesn't go away, or a pain of some type, you make an appointment with a doctor. The doctor examines you and evaluates your symptoms to make a *diagnosis*. He or she might also use blood tests and scans. A course of action is then taken designed to alleviate or remove the symptoms you presented. Often a medication is prescribed to help your body fight off the affliction. This is what we call *treatment*.

In our culture, the expectation is to consult with an expert when something goes wrong. For your car you go to a mechanic. For your body you go to a doctor. For your mind it seems less clear just where to go and what to do. Can a medical doctor help you with mental health symptoms? Did you know that depression and anxiety are problems mostly handled by primary care physicians, almost always exclusively with medication?

Before starting medication such as an antidepressant or anti-anxiety agent, a responsible diagnosis needs to be made. This, of course, is based on careful inquiry and a thorough physical examination. Could something entirely physical be causing these symptoms? Yes. For example, if your thyroid gland does not function at its full efficiency, a condition called *hypothyroidism*, you would probably feel tired, down, unmotivated, or anxious. A good physical examination by your trusted doctor is a good place to start. You may find that a medical intervention is all you need to become symptom free and this will solve your problem.

But, what if you need something more? Would talking help? Ask your doctor if he or she would recommend talk therapy.

A nice young man requested my service by presenting with the complaints of feeling very nervous and having a muscle spasm in the back of his neck that was causing him a great deal of pain. This change in him was relatively new and he was asking for a few sessions to figure things out. When asked if there was "anything different" going on in his life, he answered with a definitive "Yes." He had studied performing arts in college, participated in a local theater group, believed that he had talent, and now wanted to start a career as an actor.

This man was making plans to move west to California and was quite excited about this idea. He pointed out that he had to take this risk of moving or he would never know what the future would hold for him. He spoke about his parents being divided in their support and he did not want to let them down.

He also spoke about his ambivalence of leaving behind a job, apartment, and friends. But he was willing to do this for his future. He had saved some money, researched the physical landscape, and knew where he was going to start out. He learned well from a previous visit to California a few years prior, and was not going to make the same mistakes.

So, he was leaving a known and stable life to find out if he could make it in a less known environment with limited funds and social supports. There was a lot for him to plan and do, but he also knew that some things would just have to evolve. He was trying to have enough faith in himself to face the challenges. Is there any wonder why he was nervous and suffering from a pain in the neck?

For this young man, talking did help. After only a few sessions, the neck pain went away. He began to look more closely at his fears and question them. He decided to look at his situation with a more rational perspective. Even if he were unable to quickly turn his dream into a reality this time around, it would still not make him a failure. It would not turn him into an unworthy person to be shunned and unloved by others. It would not diminish his value as a person. This talk therapy helped to turn his risk into an adventure.

When symptoms develop, we can become overly focused on them. This makes us blindsided, unaware of what went wrong or what might've upset the applecart. Sometimes it takes another person to help us examine, refocus, and face the real issues. A friend could do it to some extent, if they feel comfortable and able. However, sometimes it is better for the struggling individual to find a therapist. This would mean commitment to a working relationship with a more objective person and a willingness to explore what is behind the pain. In truth, a professional can offer much more than a friend, helping you work through the problem with greater consistency and continuity. A therapist can also offer clinical knowledge and skills based on training, experience and best practice methods.

Marla was a young woman referred to me by her family doctor. She came to him suffering with migraine headaches, irritable bowel syndrome, and feelings of tension, anxiety, and depression. She lost ten pounds, had trouble sleeping, and felt like a wreck. She knew that she felt horrible but wasn't sure exactly why. It didn't take very long to find out that Marla was one year into her third marriage and things were not going well. They met at work and had a lovely brief courtship. She moved into his house where they were supposed to live happily ever after. He encouraged her to give up her job and stay home. She was not to worry about anything because he would take care of her.

However, things soon went sour. He started spending more and more time away from home with no explanation. He avoided talking about money and kept the financial situation close to his chest. His mood and behavior often changed for no clear reason, and then the fighting began. On several occasions he told her to "get out" and "make a plan" for herself. It was a clear message of rejection; the marriage was over for him.

She also revealed that he had a "slight imperfection," like her own father—a gambler. When turning to her mother, she received old school advice: "He's a nice guy. You may never do any better. You should stay with him for better or worse." Marla was torn apart by her love for him and couldn't handle his rejection. This was her third time on the marriage circuit. Had she learned anything? Could this be another mistake? Maybe he would come around if she only waited it out and actively showed her love and devotion.

Marla's husband never went for help despite her constant pleading. She gradually came to realize that his first love was gambling, and she was not the priority that she hoped to be. It took some time, but she eventually gave up the fantasy that love would conquer all. Though it was difficult, she had to give up the idea that, "If I love someone hard enough, they should and would love me back."

Marla eventually began to see that all her tears and emotional disturbance were not enough to break him of his addiction and turn his attention back toward her. She began to experience feelings of shame and embarrassment about her family and friends finding out. "And what about me?" she asked. "Will I be able to survive on my own? Am I a failure, a loser?" She wondered if she would ever find love again. It was another loss.

Marla showed tremendous resilience when she finally accepted that there was no going back. She was surprised to find her family and friends more supportive than she expected. She took responsibility for taking care of herself. She found an apartment and a job, and then started building an enjoyable social life. She worked hard to stop being critical of herself and was able to better accept herself as a fallible person. Therapy helped her symptoms subside and she was pleased to be feeling better.

We are not always ready for the unpleasant surprises that life brings our way. Sometimes we don't even recognize what they are until we sort out why we are not feeling well, why we are having physical or emotional symptoms. Life stressors can sometimes become overwhelming and cause us to break down. We all react to such things as a death, loss of a job, divorce, and illness. A new job or move to a new neighborhood may initially seem positive but then cause some problems.

All such transitions will have an effect on us and sometimes result in distressing symptoms. Did you know that one in five people need to seek counseling or a mental health service at some point in their lives? The good news is that most can successfully get through it and learn something valuable about themselves—they can become wiser, stronger, and happier in the long run. If you need some help, don't be shy or ashamed to ask for it. Get whatever help you need to feel better, and become better. Go ahead and live your life well!

Part II

—

Thoughts & Beliefs

5

The Power of Your Beliefs

What you think and how strong you believe it is the key to your mental health and to your overall sense of well-being. It is very much connected to what you feel and, in turn, what you do. There has been much written in the scientific and clinical literatures to show the powerful connection between beliefs, emotions, and behavior. The mind is a tricky thing and not always easy to predict. The process of taking in and evaluating information from the environment is both complicated and remarkable.

The power of beliefs was keenly demonstrated in a classic series of experiments at Yale University on obedience and authority (Milgram, 1963, 1974). Researchers asked subjects to give increasing doses of electric shock to confederates, who were presumably experiencing increasing pain as a result of those shocks. But those confederates were not really experiencing pain. Rather, they were acting as if they did, for the sake of studying how the subjects would follow the commands of a research expert.

Would study subjects abide by their moral values and stop

administering painful shocks to other human beings? Would conscience prevail over authority? It turned out that many of the subjects, thinking they were inflicting pain, continued to do so despite their personal inclination to stop. They were told to follow protocol and strongly encouraged to continue by a study expert. The expert insisted that the confederates were not really being hurt and it was very important for the study to continue in the name of science.

What could the subjects then be thinking to reconcile this contradictory experience? Subjects began to believe that the expert scientist affiliated with a prestigious institution truly knew what he was doing. They started believing that their own actions genuinely contributed to science and the good of mankind. They convinced themselves that it was okay to go on with their instructed task and set aside their initial moral beliefs.

In another study, subjects were paid either $20 or $1 to be involved in a rather mundane activity. They were then asked to rate the activity based on their thoughts about its level of interest and value (Festinger & Carlsmith, 1959). It may be a challenge to guess the results, but if you guessed the $1 group gave the better rating, then you'd be right! I would have guessed that the higher paid group ($20) would have more reason to be convinced the task had interest and value. I would consider this to be especially true of poor students. The subjects paid the lower amount, however, became more invested, saying the study held their interest. The issue became less about the influence of money and more about the activity and their own involvement. As you can see, the subjects' evaluations of the activity were based on the beliefs they developed about it. These beliefs became the basis of their motivation and reactions.

What is the lesson to be learned from these experiments? To better understand people, in general, it is important to not only look at their external situations, but to also carefully examine and trace their thinking. The power of the mind is better revealed in this way.

A young man told me his story of growing up in a rough and dangerous urban environment filled with gangs and crime. He spoke of another young man living across the hall of his tenement building. This was someone to be feared and avoided, so he thought.

"He was a bad kid with a criminal rap sheet an arm long," the man told me. He hated the way this guy walked, talked, and dressed. "He was far down on my list of people and not someone I'd call a friend."

However, "One day he stepped up and saved my sister from a gang of guys who were up to no good. They probably would have raped her."

"Did you still see him as *all* bad?" I asked.

His thoughts about this young man had changed. "This guy went up a whole lot of notches in my mind," he said.

Now, let's take a look at how thoughts have a major role in mental health and one's ability to function in the world. Suppose you were unable to get to work on time. You were always late because you had to check your electric garage door many times over. You had to make sure that the door went down and stayed down. You wound up checking that door so many times that you would end up losing your job.

Why feel so compelled to check the door? Because of intense feelings you experience, feelings of tension and anxiety causing much distress. You feel relieved by giving into the compulsion, so you continue to check the door.

What thoughts would be behind this compulsion? They might be something like this: "If I were to leave the garage door open, my house would get robbed. If my house gets robbed, I'd lose my valued possessions. I'd be violated and feel victimized. All this would be my own fault. I would be the one to blame. What a fool I'd be! I can't stand the possibility of this happening to me. How awful it would be!"

Do such thoughts seem extreme? Well they certainly are, and they form the basis of a well-known problem called *obsessive-compulsive disorder* (OCD).

Consider that this person may also feel the need to wash his hands repeatedly and be unable to remain on a work task for any length of time. His hands may get very dry, chapped, and his skin may begin to split from all the washing. Why do it? He does it because of the strong thoughts that swirl about in his head—in this case, thoughts about being unable to tolerate exposure to germs. He may also think about a long painful illness, and even death. If he does not wash his hands, he will continue to suffer the strong feelings of emotional distress. This is someone who truly needs help.

Not everyone, however, has to line up for a therapist's couch. How often do you watch a baseball player step up to the plate wearing a favorite article of clothing or crossing his chest before getting up to bat? The thought of this particular ritual is that "It will bring me luck." The athlete might even believe this and gain more confidence to play better. It may be a bit crazy but it's not really harmful. It doesn't get in his way or cause serious disturbance. The point is that people of all walks of life believe in all kinds of things. We are all a little bit nutty if you look closely at some of the things we think. But this doesn't mean that we are all mentally ill.

So how do you know when it's time to seek some extra help for the beliefs you hold? When your thoughts strongly and consistently get in the way of living life, then it's time to consider therapy. When you begin to see your thoughts driving you to do something that doesn't seem normal, then it's time to consider therapy. When your thoughts interfere with your ability to function, then it's time to consider therapy. These are the times when you need help.

Mattie came to me with a serious gambling problem. He was fascinated by the sights and sounds of the nearby casino and convinced himself that these were "exciting" and "entertaining." Every time his friends or family came to visit, he would take them to play the slot machines. Each episode of playing the slots would result in a loss of anywhere between three hundred to five hundred dollars. He enjoyed it so much that he wiped out his entire savings account of over twenty thousand dollars.

First Mattie would scope out the casino for what he thought might be a "hot machine." Either it was played for what seemed to be a long time by someone else, or it was just standing there waiting to pay out "the big win." If the machine didn't pay out to his satisfaction over a period of time, he moved over to another machine requiring more dollars on the bet. Even though each play was independent and the slot machines kept having the same low chance of winning, Mattie kept telling himself, "It's due to pay out. My time is coming."

His time did come—to feel let down and depressed when he failed to win. This time he was telling himself, "What a fool and loser I am to let this happen!"

Every emotion and behavior has a thought component behind it. If you pass a friend and she doesn't stop to say hello, you might quickly feel angry by saying to yourself something like this: "What a self-absorbed snob! She should be more polite and social." But if you took the time to gather more information, you might find out that she was heading for an important meeting, had a lot on her mind, and just didn't see you at that time. The "snub" was not intentional, but an oversight with no malicious intent at all.

Like many humans, you may have a tendency to think toward the negative and this could lead to a negative feeling. In turn, it may end up with a negative behavior, such as a decision to ignore her the next time your paths cross. The good news is that with a little practice, you have the ability to identify your own thoughts and look at how they work for or against you.

You also have the ability to look more carefully at situations and evaluate them more objectively. This is better than always following your initial misperceptions.

Does this mean that you can think yourself into emotional and behavioral disturbance? That's right! And, if you can think yourself into it, then you can also think yourself out of it! Pretty simple, huh? The concept is pretty simple, but implementing it is not so easy.

Turning back to Mattie, he thought of his gambling troubles as having "fallen deep into a ditch." This meant he would have to work very hard to pull himself out. Can you envision this? Telling yourself over and over again distorted and erroneous thoughts, as Mattie did, would surely lead to disturbed emotions and behaviors. In Mattie's case, his beliefs were considered *magical thinking* about having luck and having a good feeling about the "one armed bandits" he played. It fed his compulsive addiction to gambling.

These thoughts were embedded in Mattie's mind by a process of *self-indoctrination*. Before therapy, he wasn't aware of how his thoughts contributed to his addiction. He knew that he had troubles and that was about it.

For Mattie as for most of us, it is not always immediately clear how we develop these problems. But don't fret about it or lose hope. Like a splinter under your skin causing discomfort, you will find it, work with it, and eventually pick it out. You will probably need some help with this process, and it won't be entirely painless. But with hard work, commitment, and perseverance the end result will lead to much relief.

6

Removing the Splinter

When you believe in something that is true and it supports your goals in life, it generally contributes to good mental health and social functioning. Your thoughts alone may not be enough, however, because thoughts can be weak. It is the *strength* of your thoughts that really makes the difference—it's what makes them a part of your *belief system*.

For example, if you grew up being told over and over again that you are "no good and will never amount to anything," it is likely that this message will internalize into your psyche and damage your self-worth. This personal assault can become part of your belief system and continue to haunt you to this very day.

On the other hand, if you grew up receiving a nurturing message, the likelihood is that the opposite belief will fill your brain. You are more apt to think of yourself as "a unique, smart, and talented person, capable of being successful, and making positive contributions to the world." Wow! What a great message to keep in mind, whether you are fully aware of it or not. The message is always there but not always conscious. It is a part of you, irrespective of gender, race or social class. It is part of your belief system—the strong thoughts you have that form your self-esteem.

A young single mother came to me feeling depressed and especially unhappy about her weight. She usually shopped in women's large size clothing shops and was fashionably dressed. She kept up her personal hygiene and tried hard to give herself the respect she deserved. However, she felt stuck by her weight problem and couldn't seem to motivate herself to change. She wanted to join Weight Watchers, slow down her eating, and get regular exercise.

"It's my mother," she explained. Although she knew at some level that mother loved her, it was difficult to take the "hard-nosed criticism I had to suffer through all my life." Her mother would harshly point out to her that her weight was a huge burden. If she only dropped the pounds, maybe she would find a man and not have to bear the loneliness of single parenting.

Although she agreed that it would be in her best interest to drop the pounds for reasons of health and self-image, her anger at her mother prevented her from reaching this goal. To lose the weight and move on with her life would give her mother too much satisfaction. As the mother–daughter conflict played out, they both suffered. "Why must she (mother) be that way?" she cried out in our sessions. This lovely young woman put her life on hold because she insisted that her mother change.

Isn't that often the case? People get stuck and emotionally disturbed by insisting and holding onto the thought that someone else has to make a change. This becomes the requirement before they can do anything for themselves. Good luck with that thought! You can be in a struggle of this kind for the rest of your life.

A lot of relationships and marriages fail for this very reason. One partner insists that the other partner make a change, and "He ought to know what that change is."

"Have you told him?" I often ask.

"No."

"Then how could he possibly know?" Placing all your happiness into someone else's hands is a big mistake. Even if that other person knows what you expect, he or she may be unable or unwilling to give you what you want. Aren't *you* responsible for *you*? Maybe this wasn't the case when you were a child, a time when you were dependent on your parents or guardians to love and nurture you. However, as an adult, now is the time for you to pick up on that task, take better care of yourself, take charge of your happiness, and do it right. Don't make the blunder of looking outside of yourself!

To ensure successful therapy, let's be clear. Whatever you think and say to yourself, your beliefs, have *everything* to do with your mood state and actions. If you haven't already learned this from reading the previous chapters, I'll say it again: Your beliefs affect your feelings and behaviors.

Your personal world is based on your individual thoughts and beliefs. From the time you wake up in the morning until the time you put your head back on the pillow at night, your thoughts and beliefs are guiding you. They may also be buzzing around in your head while you sleep. You may be thinking about what the day will be like and that you better push yourself out of bed to get started with your morning routines. You may be thinking about your appointment today or an important task at work. This thinking or *self-talk* may not seem to be in your awareness, as it is quite automatic. However, if you look for it, you will find it there.

But what about medications, body chemistry, and environment? Yes, all those things do have an impact on your life as well, and will certainly be considered as part of your therapy. When interventions are made in these areas, you think to yourself, "That was needed. I feel better. What a relief!" Confirming or denying the benefits of these interventions is a form of

self-evaluation based on a cognitive process. You come to recognize these changes as part of your thoughts—what you end
up saying to yourself and what you eventually come to believe.

Let's talk for a moment about the *placebo effect*. Although
various medications are researched and designed to alter body
chemistry, it is common knowledge among medical professionals that any given pill will work better if the patient is more
hopeful about its results. This is why doctors are taught to gain
the confidence of their patients by having a good bedside manner. This is also why drug manufacturers choose a size, shape,
and color of pill most pleasant and amenable to the patient. It
improves adherence to a medication regimen.

Thirty years ago, when I was working in a public mental
health clinic, a middle-aged woman came in complaining of
generalized anxiety. The wise psychiatrist on call decided to
not subject her to a habit-forming anti-anxiety medication. He
wrote a prescription for "Obecalp" instead. If you can't recognize this medication, try spelling it backwards. He told her that
this was a highly effective drug designed to help her get better
quickly and stay calm.

It worked miracles! In the follow-up visit, the patient came
in feeling happy and expressing gratitude. She wondered what
she would have done without it. Nowadays, it is considered
highly unethical to practice in this way. The patient needs to be
fully informed about the treatment, the expected therapeutic
outcome, and any possible side effects.

The counterpart to the placebo is less known. It is called the
nocebo effect. Here there is a negative process of belief and, as
you may have guessed, the person taking the pill ends up with a
variety of problematic symptoms. So, it can go either way, and
your outlook makes much of the difference.

While taking a pill could be helpful, you may not find it
to be a permanent solution. Like removing a splinter, getting
rid of emotional disturbance and solving real-life problems in-

volves a good deal of commitment and hard work. You will be doing this work inside and outside of therapy sessions.

A valuable therapeutic approach that addresses the importance of beliefs is called *rational emotive behavior therapy* (REBT), developed by renowned psychologist Albert Ellis in the 1950's after he discovered that psychoanalysis with his clients did not satisfactorily do the job. Even though they were accepting dynamic interpretations, their symptoms and emotional disturbances did not subside. He concluded that his methods needed to change and that most people would do better with a more active approach. For more effective results, the therapist could take a more directive stance, and the client could be a more active participant in the therapy. Ellis spoke of three important insights:

1. Your *irrational beliefs* about people (including yourself) and events are the cause of your disturbance.
2. You continue to upset yourself by telling yourself these irrational beliefs over and over again—you cling to them.
3. You can overcome your disturbance by working very hard to challenge, debate, dispute and act against these irrational beliefs.

As I have already mentioned, self-talk is automatic and such thoughts may not be immediately in your awareness. Humans, however, are high in the evolutionary hierarchy, and what this means is that they have an extraordinary ability to *think about their own thinking*. In short, as part of being human, you have the power to identify the thoughts that lead you to feel and act upset!

Try finding these thoughts and putting them into words or sentences. Once you have accomplished this task, you can then work on understanding them better. You can look at their rationality and determine if they make good sense. You will probably need help with this but that's why you decided to enter therapy. When you recognize that your disturbing thoughts are not rational, you become empowered to make significant changes. You will begin to realize that these unhealthy thoughts are not helping you to feel well, act well, or stay well.

Therapy will help you get better. And it can best do so by helping you find answers to the following questions: What healthy alternative thoughts can you put into place to tear down those disturbing irrational ones? How strongly are you working on believing your new rational thoughts and incorporating this healthier point of view into your life? Did you know that it is better to act on these new rational thoughts, even if you don't yet fully believe them?

In essence, therapy will help you develop a new outlook on life. And it will help you practice behaviors that are consistent with your new outlook. Sometimes it's hard to give up older thoughts and behaviors. But while it may initially be out of your comfort zone to think and act in different ways, it is necessary to do this and stick with it! Only then can you expect to gain the most out of therapy.

7

The Content of
Your Thoughts

Now that we have established that thoughts make a big difference in how you feel and what you do, let's take a look at their content. Remember, the strength of your belief in these thoughts makes all the difference. Later, after you have learned more about identifying some of your own thoughts, you can try rating your degree of belief in them on a ten-point scale. You may be surprised at how much you hold onto the same irrational thoughts that lead you into emotional disturbance.

So we know that irrational thoughts aren't good for you. But just what are those irrational thoughts that make you and keep you disturbed?

Demand versus Preference

Albert Ellis and his colleagues have helped many people find and correct their self-sabotaging thoughts. One type of thought that they were asked to search for was the demanding *should, must* or *have to* statement. Having such *demand thoughts* leads to feeling terribly upset when frustrated, resulting in emotions such as anger, rage, anxiety, or depression. Such thoughts are unhealthy because you are putting undue pressure on yourself—blame for past mistakes or absolute requirements for future achievements—that can make you feel miserable. It's an unhealthy negative feeling.

On the other hand, thoughts of *want, preference,* or *desire* for things to go your way, lead to a healthier type of negative feeling when frustrated. You might feel annoyance, disappointment, or sadness. These are more manageable and make coping easier. Such healthier beliefs are called *preference thoughts.*

Hence, if a *want* becomes a *demand,* you will get into deep emotional trouble when things don't work out as you expected. Simply said, when a *desire* becomes a *require,* you will end up feeling it intensely and this becomes your emotional disturbance.

Do you get it? Let's take a sample situation to better understand this. If your boyfriend rejected you after a year of dating, what would you be thinking? You might think: "After a year of loyalty and devotion, how dare he do this to me. He *must* not hurt me in this way!" Can you feel the intensity of your emotions build? As difficult as it may seem, if you were not overtaken by the demanding *must,* you would be less upset and cope better. You could alternatively think to yourself: "I am disappointed that this didn't work out, as I would have *preferred.* It is too bad. Maybe I'm better off finding out now than later."

The situation about which you create beliefs has a specific name; Ellis called it the *activating event.* It is usually an external situation, often an obstacle you experience in everyday life. It can be the stress of an upcoming job interview, a failed test, or a loss of a friend. It can also be an internal event such as a repetitive distressing thought or image that intrusively enters your mind. It can even be an uncomfortable physical sensation.

The natural human response is to evaluate the activating event. As in the case above, when you look at the rejection as merely an unfortunate situation—"it's too bad" or "so what, these things happen"—it then becomes a manageable event and you can better cope with the appropriate negative feelings of disappointment and sadness.

Awfulizing or Catastrophizing

What happens if you think of an activating event as *awful, horrible,* or *terrible*? That's when you go back to insisting to yourself over and over again that it *should not* or *must not* happen, causing you to get all worked up and disturbed. You get yourself into a tizzy and find yourself unable to get out of it! As a kid, your mother may have told you not to make a mountain out of a molehill. She was trying to get you to change your thinking about the situation so that you would feel better.

Unfortunately, bad things *do* happen and it makes sense to react with normal negative emotions. However, too frequently those bad life experiences are exaggerated in your head to be worse than they really are—and voila, you develop intense negative emotions as a result. Back to our example, if rejection by that boyfriend makes you feel extremely depressed rather than the more appropriate emotions of disappointment and sadness, then you are having an unhealthy and extreme overreaction. Ellis called this *awfulizing.* Sometimes it's also referred to as *catastrophizing.*

These two terms don't normally appear in the English language. "Awful" is an adjective and "catastrophe" is a noun. But Ellis creatively modified these terms into verbs because he considered the thinking process to be an action—something that you *do.* When you turn an unfortunate situation into an "awful" one in your thoughts, you are engaging in an action—you make yourself sick with disturbed emotions.

These thought processes are quite automatic and you don't even realize that you are engaging in them at the time. Therapy can help you become aware of your unhealthy thoughts and how they came about. And therapy also can help you learn how to develop the power to undo those bad thoughts and replace them with healthy ones. With motivation, conscious effort, and a better understanding of the process, you can catch yourself in the act of awfulizing or catastrophizing, and you can learn to stop doing it.

This is certainly a more sensible and rational plan than continuing to make yourself miserable. Has your misery changed things for the better? Of course not! In essence, viewing the world in an awful or catastrophic way is a distortion of reality. Therapy can help you change such distortions.

The Unfairness of It All

"But I'm a nice person and I do all the right things. It's just not fair!" Have you heard yourself saying these things? Let's get real! Who guaranteed that if you followed all the rules and you were a good person, the world would always give you pleasant rewards? Why do you believe that the world must always be fair? Look around. Think about it. Is it true? Of course it's not true.

How many good people do you know who have suffered the loss and grief of a loved one or the pain and helplessness of a debilitating physical illness? How many good people do you know who have lost their jobs and livelihoods because of a struggling economy? All these events were outside of their control and clearly unfair. So, as difficult as this may seem to grasp, the world we live in is not always fair, and that's the full truth. It is a world filled with both good and bad, with no guarantees about fairness, even if you are a good person and do all the right things. No matter how much you insist otherwise, this insistence will only make you deeply frustrated and painfully upset. You can scream as loud as you want. But my advice is to take a deep breath and accept the world as it is.

I'm not saying that when bad things happen you should like it. I'm not saying that you need to sit back and be powerless about it either. There may be things you *can* do to make the situation better. However, I am saying that endless complaining and bellyaching about how bad the world is when things do go wrong will only keep you bound up, feeling victimized and unable to live a meaningful life.

Accepting the world for what it is does not mean giving up responsibility for your thoughts and behavior. On the contrary, most of us would agree with the philosophy that we are here to contribute and make the world a better place. As you know, when you follow appropriate societal rules, you usually get rewarded. It generally feels good to do the right thing and follow your good conscience. If your behavior stays within the law, you will likely not get into legal entanglements or confined to a jail cell. If you act in a loving way to your husband or wife, you will likely get love and affection in return. If you give gifts or participate in charitable endeavors, you will likely feel happy just by giving to others and you may be recognized and appreciated for your efforts.

However, let me repeat, don't expect that things in this world will always go your way. Try to make your life a lot healthier and more meaningful by taking the right attitude and doing the right things, but also try to remember the importance of being flexible and accepting of reality. This means having the courage to live your life to its fullest and taking the good with the bad.

Can't-Stand-It-Itis

If you accept the things that you know are unlikely to change, you demonstrate a trait that most humans instinctively have and can further develop. It's called *resilience*. For many, it is a bit of a struggle because of their strong demanding and awfulizing. Their beliefs get caught up in the thought that they "can't stand it" and they tend to fall apart if things don't go their way. Yes, when life hits hard with heavy obstacles, they think to themselves that "it's too much" and that they are just "too weak." This stuff is damaging and makes for severe emotional disturbance. Ellis and his colleagues have called it *can't-stand-it-itis*. If you have this problem, you view yourself as unable to handle stress.

When an activating event or stressor comes your way, you really have no other choice but to face it and handle it. Certainly it is not what you bargained for and you would prefer to have life be much easier. But, is it always your call? You surely may not like it, but what real proof is there that you just can't handle it?

"Look at how upset I am," you say. "Isn't that proof enough?"

Not quite. That only proves you are facing and handling it poorly. Suppose you truly believed that you had the strength to move forward and the stressor was indeed difficult but not insurmountable. Would you still be as upset? Of course not! Can you now see that the can't-stand-it-itis came first? It came before your so-called meltdown. And, by the way, aren't you still around to complain about how miserable you were? You really haven't melted away. Isn't that proof that you *can* stand it, though you clearly didn't like it?

Blaming Yourself & Others

If you are late for a job interview and didn't get the job... If you didn't study for a test and failed it... If your lover drops you for someone else... You can probably think of 100 more possible things that can go wrong. Do you ever think to yourself, "What a schmuck I am?" Do you ever blame and condemn yourself? Do you mentally beat yourself up to the point of being terribly upset or emotionally disturbed? Do you do this toward someone else or perhaps the world in general?

These thoughts of *blame* are all ways to contribute to your own emotional pain. They are all irrational, self-sabotaging, and hurtful—not a good model for coping. If your lover took off with someone else, does this mean that you are not lovable or a good person? Should you be the one to fully blame for what happened? Is he really "a no-good son of a bitch who deserves to rot in hell?" Are you?

With some help, you can come to recognize that he may have some character flaws, perhaps a deficit in sensitivity and an inability to remain faithful. But how does the blaming and condemnation help you to get through, to cope with adversity and to minimize your suffering? It doesn't. It only creates hate, anger, and depression.

Hate and anger of another person happens because of your blame toward them. You see them as the cause of all your problems. Depression, on the other hand, may come in the form of self-blame, self-deprecation, or self hate. That's a pretty strong dose of unnecessary cognitive energy.

Overstating the Past or Future

Depression may also come in the form of self-pity. You start thinking to yourself that this "terrible" event "*always* happens and will *always* happen to me!" Such *overstating of the past or future* comes with a deep internal sigh and only one conclusion—"poor me." You start feeling sorry for yourself, and this can go on for a very long time. Maybe forever!

Is there a more sensible way of looking at it? Is there a way to undo this emotional mess you've gotten yourself into? Of course there is! You can begin by questioning the truth and validity of these negative thoughts you've been stubbornly holding onto. Do these terrible things really *always* happen to you? Isn't that a bit of an exaggeration? How can you truly know that it will always happen to you? Are you able to predict the future? Do you have some special superhuman power to see what's ahead?

If you do, please let me know. Together we'll be able to do wonders and also get very rich.

8

The ABC's of REBT

Now that you are familiar with how beliefs affect emotions and behavior, let's look at a simple model to use as a tool for analyzing these beliefs and working on change. The *ABC Model*, the guiding framework for REBT, was developed by Albert Ellis and found to be quite useful over the years for many people actively engaged in solving their problems.

Before presenting this model and giving a working example, I want to remind you of a couple of important points. First, the goal is to become more rational in your thinking, feeling, and acting. Rational means being able to think, feel, and act in ways that contribute to your wellness and ability to function. It helps you to get where you want to go and feel the way you want to feel. To be irrational is the very opposite and keeps you stuck in disturbance and poor mental health. Second, rational does not mean always feeling good. It's just not humanly possible to go through life without experiencing negative events and, in turn, having some negative feelings. However, it is all a matter of degree. As I have said before, sadness does not have to become depression, and concern does not have to become anxiety.

Morris was a fifty-three-year-old man who came to my office with his wife. She was concerned about her husband because he was depressed. "He's just not himself," she said. He admitted to feeling down in the dumps, irritable, anxious, not sleeping or eating well, and at times felt that he just wanted to break out in tears. In fact, he did so at his doctor's appointment and then again with me.

After some discussion, we quickly got to the root of his problem. His mood was seriously impacted by the distressing thoughts he held about a very disappointing situation. He had been transferred at work. Although he had been comfortable in the job of trucking supervisor in charge of his company's transportation needs, his employer recently moved him to a position overseeing production of the machine workers at the plant. There was no change in salary but it did affect his schedule by occasionally having to work later shifts. He thought of the new job as unsatisfying and having to "babysit" the factory workers. He had not been consulted about this change, strongly disagreed with it, and felt betrayed by his employer. Unfortunately, he saw it as a demotion and the change in job duties constituted a loss for him.

The ABC Model

Morris took well to the REBT approach and was a willing participant in identifying the three elements of the ABC Model in his case: (A) the situation that began it all—the *activating event*, (B) his beliefs about the activating event—his *automatic thoughts*, and (C) the *consequences* of those thoughts—his feelings and behaviors. He agreed to do *homework* exercises, which helped him to develop and apply coping skills to feel better. He also actively worked at challenging and modifying his irrational beliefs to actually get better. Here are Morris's ABC's:

(A) Activating Event:

Unwanted job transfer.

(B) Beliefs About the Activating Event:

(1) Rational Beliefs (wants, desires, preferences).

- I don't like this change. I really want my old job back.
- It would have been better if they consulted with me.
- It's unfortunate that it happened.
- How annoying and inconvenient.

(2) Irrational Beliefs (demands, awfulizing, I can't stand it, blame/downing/punishment):

- After all I have done for them, how could these bastards have done this to me? They deserve to rot in hell!
- They should have treated me fairly by keeping me in my old job.
- It's awful that they didn't!
- Others will think less of me because I've been demoted.
- Maybe they'll be right!
- I can't stand this new job!
- Work will never be good for me!

(C) Consequences of Beliefs (emotional, behavioral).

(1) Desirable Emotions:

- Disappointment.
- Sadness.
- Frustration.

(2) Desirable Behaviors:

- Willingness to move forward.
- Try to change the situation by making it more favorable.
- Work on better accepting situation by acknowledging the positives.

(3) Undesirable Emotions:

- Depression.
- Anger.
- Anxiety.
- Shame.
- Feelings of Worthlessness.

(4) Undesirable Behavior:

- Immobilized.
- Stuck.
- Overwhelmed.
- Pessimistic.

So the above might be a lot to digest, but hopefully you can see how breaking down Morris's situation into its basic ABC elements might prove helpful in therapy. By understanding what these elements are, especially the beliefs he holds about the activating event, we can begin to move toward disputing those beliefs. Next, we'll see how we did so in Morris's case.

Disputing or Debating Irrational Beliefs

As part of therapy, after we have a good understanding of the automatic thoughts that contribute to Morris's distress, it's time to look at each more closely and challenge them. Some questions I gently posed to Morris included: What evidence exists that they should or must have treated you differently? Is it really awful that they changed your job? How does this change make you less of a person? What is the proof that you can't stand it? How could you know that work will never be good for you?

As you might suspect, these questions provided excellent fodder for discussion in therapy. And as we did, Morris began to question his own irrational beliefs about the job transfer. This resulted in three broad categories of change for him.

Cognitive Change

Over time, these are the new beliefs that Morris developed, after challenging his initial irrational automatic thoughts:

- I would have preferred to be treated differently, but there is no real evidence that they should not or must not have done this because of what I wanted. They are not bastards but businessmen, and they have every right to make their business decisions, even if I don't agree with them. It's not personal and I'm much better off not looking at it that way.
- While it's not what I wanted and it will be a major inconvenience for me, nothing really makes it awful. I know that the world is not always fair, and that is often true in business, as well. The more I insist otherwise, the more disturbed I will make myself.
- Even if others think less of me, I don't have to do the same. The people who love and care about me will continue to do so and give me support. This job shift did not come with a salary reduction and is not really a demotion. Even if it were, I can still respect myself.
- Though I don't like it, I can certainly stand this change. It won't literally kill me and I still have a job to support my family.
- I can't really predict the future. Perhaps I can be more open to new experiences and appreciate whatever benefits

may come with this job change. It's not that bad!

Emotional Change

As a result of these new thoughts, Morris began feeling differently, and feeling much better. Although still sometimes frustrated, he thought about his frustration in a new way. Here are some of his new feelings:

- Disappointed and sorrowful but not depressed.
- Frustrated but not angry.
- Concerned but not anxious.
- Self-accepting and not self-deprecating.

Behavioral Change

The important changes Morris made in his irrational thinking also led to change in his behavior. He began to take positive action to change his situation. Here are some of the new behaviors that Morris experienced:

- Moving forward in the new job with a more open mind.
- Discussing with his boss the reason for the change.
- Considering and applying for alternative opportunities within and outside of the company.
- Enjoying family and social life, even with some scheduling inconveniences.

Uncovering the ABC's for your own activating events, and then developing a plan to dispute your irrational thoughts doesn't happen overnight. It takes time and practice. And as you know, many irrational beliefs are automatic thoughts, meaning you're not always immediately aware of them. So therapy can help facilitate the process for you.

There are also many professional worksheets that can help, and your therapist might assign them as homework for you to complete between sessions. *The Rational Self Help Form* provides an excellent framework and worksheet to help you think through how you get yourself disturbed and how you can get yourself out of it. If you are like me, writing it down and having a visual tool works wonders. It is a learning process and your active involvement is crucial.

There are other versions of this homework form to make it less cumbersome and more user friendly. *The Daily Record of Dysfunctional Thoughts* also records the situation, emotions, automatic thoughts, rational response, and outcome. Moreover, it adds a rating component with a 100-point scale to help identify intensity of beliefs and emotions. *Negative Thoughts & Challenges* is another option, giving a skeletal approach to both of these forms by simply dividing the page in two with negative thoughts on one side and alternative challenges on the other. It works too!

Try out these helpful written tools to see how they work for you. Bring them into your sessions to ask your therapist for further guidance and advice regarding their use. You can find more information about these forms at WilliamLKnupp.com.

When you don't feel well, it can be difficult to find the motivation to implement the ABC Model. You will probably want to wait until you have some creative energy to jump into any of these homework assignments. However, sometimes you need to just push yourself to write things down. You can always ask your therapist for further clarification regarding your homework and any additional forms.

Once the window of opportunity arises, don't wait too long. You may just find yourself idle and procrastinating. That will make matters worse! When considering the use of these forms, it's better to put something in writing without worrying about how well you're doing it. Throw your perfectionism aside. Take your time and don't expect yourself to get it all done in one sitting.

Remember, don't be too hard on yourself, and do take things one step at a time. No journey can be successfully taken without keeping this in mind. Welcome to your new journey!

Part III

—

The People in Your Life

9

Relationships

No guidebook for therapy can be complete without some discussion of relationships. However, this is a rather complicated task because there are so many types of relationships, and with these come so many different expectations of what constitutes a desirable relationship. A *model of concentric social circles* would be helpful in conceptualizing some important ideas. Let's start simply by imagining three circles, one inside of the other. The outer circle has space representing people in the outer community. The middle circle represents people who are acquaintances or co-workers. Finally, the core inner circle will contain close friends and family.

Your Outer Circle

People in the *outer circle* or community run about their tasks of living by doing whatever you do. Many go to work, see that their kids go off to school, stop for some last minute groceries, and finally get home to eat dinner, watch television, read a book, and get a good night's sleep. The next day it's back to the same routines. If they are particularly energetic and self-disciplined, they'll find some time for exercise and go off to the gym.

Others are less fortunate, where they may suffer from an addiction, disabling disease, unemployment, homelessness, or numerous other problems. Some are young and some are old. Whatever their situation, these are the people living in your wider community—in your town, city, county, state, and country. You don't necessarily know these people though you may recognize some of them or heard of them. Whatever the connection, we are all bound together by community, culture, and laws. These are the relationships of our outer circle.

Early in our lives we begin to learn the rules and norms of society. We continue learning as we grow older and become more refined in our behavior. Those of us that "fit in" will be considered socially appropriate. They will know what is expected and what to do. They will have adequate social skills. They will be accepting of the group and the group will be accepting of them. Their behavior will bring no particular attention their way and they will carry on as normal everyday individuals.

There are some people, however, who will stand out in our society. This is because of exceptional talents, achievements, or special deeds. On the other hand, the individual who defies social order—the rebel—will also be a standout. We learn about these outliers in the community by being affected by them in some way or by hearing about their activities in the media. The community at large prepares for these outliers by developing and maintaining necessary facilities and institutions. For the creative and intellectual types, they are rewarded with theaters, galleries, museums, and universities. For the antisocial types they are dealt with by a comprehensive legal system involving police organizations, courts and prisons. These systems are meant for the good of all the people in the community.

Our relationships with people in the outer social circle are very limited by definition. Paths may cross, eyes may meet, and impressions may form. But overall you spend very little time thinking about them from that moment on. Mutual communication or interpersonal contact is sparse. There are no clear emotional connections and therefore no true or meaningful relationships. It is a "sea of fish" and you are just one of them swimming along.

Your Middle Circle

The *middle circle* of our model, however, represents the people who are one step closer to you. These are your acquaintances or distant friends. You know each other a little better and wouldn't hesitate to stop on the street or in the mall to say hello. Unlike the superficial interpersonal contacts of the outer social group, your emotional energy is directed toward greater attachment. These are the people who have shared experiences with you, perhaps as neighbors, fellow workers, volunteers, or a friend of a friend.

I remember cheering with other parents on the sidelines of soccer matches and little league baseball games when my kids were playing on the field. These shared experiences made it quite enjoyable with good memories and mild attachments. Isn't it interesting, though, how we rarely use the word "acquaintance" to introduce others? If I was sitting next to and chatting with Mr. B and my wife came over, I'd say, "This is Mr. B. His son is playing second base." I might even say, "This is my *friend* Mr. B."

However, what's wrong with simply saying, "This is Mr. B., an *acquaintance* of mine"? Is it awkward? We certainly tend to be rather loose with the word "friend." In what context is that individual a friend? Does that person occupy your middle or inner circle?

In our current high tech world of computers and social media, the term "friend" is broadly used. We use Facebook to view postings and send messages, but our lack of clarity regarding the true social and emotional connection continues to exist. Such is the nature of the English language in its everyday practical use. It doesn't matter whether it's on the ball field, computer, or smartphone.

The model I present of concentric social circles comes in handy when working with your therapist on matters of relationships and social connectedness. A young single mother came to me for help with depression, loneliness, and body image problems. She was a bit overweight but exaggerated the importance of how she looked and was quick to be self-deprecating. She usually kept to herself and this social isolation only made matters worse.

When asked about her usual activities, she told about taking her daughter several times per week for a class in gymnastics. There she would meet other mothers who were quietly sitting around and politely waiting for their own daughters to finish the class. She was encouraged to make a realistic plan for herself and to actively do something constructive to work on her problems. An interesting idea popped into her head—this waiting around in the gym was really an opportunity. Why not seize the moment? She could take this time to use the rest of the facility to start walking for exercise. She could also invite the other mothers along to socialize while walking. She needed to take a social risk and, to her surprise, the suggestion was warmly welcomed by some of the other mothers. This response helped her to feel more empowered, and satisfied a desire to belong to a social group. It moved some people closer into her middle circle, and she eventually developed a couple of friends.

Before delving into the inner circle, I want to first say a few more words about relationships at the workplace. Although work requires individual responsibility, many work settings operate by some form of team approach. Because of this, one needs to get a bit closer to other people. It helps to get to really know your co-workers' strengths and weaknesses. The rules, hierarchy, and politics of the specific work venue all need to be taken into account. Discipline, order, and cooperation are important components to get the job done. A positive attitude, including tolerance of peers and other workers, contributes greatly to the emotional environment, keeping up morale, motivation and energy. These factors all influence job satisfaction and productivity. The more complicated the work task, the more need there is for group cohesiveness. Again, this means getting to know your co-workers better and being attuned to each other.

Co-workers are naturally part of the middle circle, and some of them may even get closer, nearer to the inner circle where they can justifiably be considered as close friends. But the inner circle remains well guarded by most people. Deciding to bring someone closer to you becomes a process that is not always a conscious event and there tends to be a natural protective ambivalence that is part of our human makeup. It is not unusual to want to hold back and not be sure of how close to get with someone until you are convinced of their social compatibility and whether or not you feel "safe" with that person.

In the next chapter we'll deal with your closest of relationships—those in your inner circle.

10

Your Inner Circle

Who is in your *inner circle*? These are the people you hold close. They are your good friends, close family members, and partner or soul mate. These relationships are based on positive feelings, trust, confidence, loyalty, respect, safety, and nurturance. These qualities are developed over time by mutual experiences and periods of self-disclosure. These are the building blocks of intimacy. Again, the people who make up your inner circle are considered to be your most trusted friends and "loved ones."

Friends in your inner circle often know a great deal about your personal life, habits, preferences, and values. Time spent with friends is usually for social and recreational reasons, but the inner circle is also there for emotional support to cheer for you when you are challenged and to help hold you up when things are not going well. They are confidantes and sounding boards during periods of difficulty. They assist when you need a helping hand with a project or they may even join you in a business venture.

Once a friend is in your inner circle, your closeness may be similar to that of a family member. A "best friend" may end up in your own mind as even closer, more reliable, and more trust-worthy than a blood relative. Families have been known to accept friends into their inner circles by stretching role definitions and system boundaries. With encouragement from parents, a family friend may be called by the honorary title of "aunt" or "uncle" by the kids.

Love, an umbrella term applied to your inner circle, is expressed differently for different people. The boundaries of one type of relationship does not necessarily match another, and shouldn't. For example, love for a sibling is not expressed the same as love for a spouse. Similarly, love for a parent is not shown the same as love for a child. The social and cultural rules are very clear and different in each of these relationships. These rules make up the boundaries that guide behavior within our society. The violation of these boundaries results in a great deal of tension, confusion, conflict, imbalance and disturbance for the individuals involved. This is what upsets the "apple cart." It leads families and friends into serious trouble.

So, how do we learn rules and appropriate boundaries? How do we know how to behave with those in our inner circle? Some of this comes by just living—we take it all in as children. Teaching children how to act is one of the main tasks of adult parents in a young family. Parental skills become a reflection of their own upbringing and therefore generational patterns emerge. When problems develop, we can frequently trace it back to a previous generation of poor parenting and family dysfunction.

Both mother and father originally come together for love, intimacy, and companionship. Sometimes there are other agendas, however, such as remaining in the same social class or avoiding the dread of a lifetime of loneliness. Separation from one's own parents usually leads to the building of a career and family life. The goal is to make a mark in this world and to create the next generation.

Most humans have a built in mechanism for this, a natural instinct to propagate. When our children are born, we have the next generation of nuclear family as part of our inner circle. An important task of new parents is to teach the dependent children how to function and become responsible productive adults in society—to once again follow the life cycle as already described. Parents do this by guiding, training, and modeling in a safe, caring, and nurturing environment.

When parents lose sight of these responsibilities there is serious disruption. The family system breaks down, which is usually characterized by a family member exhibiting emotional or behavioral difficulty. A child, for example, may start doing poorly in school, act out and disrespect authority. Another family member may develop a case of anxiety or depression. The parenting couple may find dissatisfaction with each other and wonder, "What happened to our marriage?" A mother may seek out a family therapist while in deep despair to announce, "My family is falling apart!"

Holding your partner close and dear is a basic value that feeds the relationship and sustains the very core of family life. It supports emotional health and keeps the family as a strong and viable system able to successfully meet all its needs—that is, to satisfy its biological and social goals. This is not always easy to do and it involves a lot of hard work. The challenges are certainly there and barriers will need to be overcome. The next chapter will further discuss some of these barriers and review important concepts to meet these challenges.

11

Barriers to Intimate Relationships

What gets in the way of a healthy and loving relationship with your partner or spouse? Now this is not rocket science, and most of you can probably make a list just as valid as the one I'm going to give you. However, it is still important to take some time to look at these problem areas and think about which ones, if not all, apply to you. This is especially true if you are thinking about entering therapy hoping to make a change in your relationship as a couple.

Some people come into therapy after enduring stress and dissatisfaction for many years. Too many! They point out how unhappy they are in their relationships, though somehow they developed ways to "stick it out" and not confront the real issues of their everyday situation. Some share the same roof but avoid dealing with each other as much as possible, essentially living separate lives. They may sweep the problems under the rug and put up a good front for their neighbors and themselves. But, if these problems are not dealt with, will they go away? Do they disappear? Does it really make for a happier life to just ignore their existence?

You may think "to each his own" and "leave well enough alone." You worry that digging under the surface might unearth more serious problems and this could likely lead to further disruption, instability, and discomfort. This keeps you covered, maintaining a sense of protectiveness and resistance to entering therapy. You seem to instinctively know that the dysfunction is dormant, like a sleeping dragon that can be dangerous if you choose to wake it up and face it.

But aren't you already facing it in some way? After all, why did you consider coming into therapy in the first place? Something must be going very wrong for you to feel this level of pain, dissatisfaction, and turmoil. Are you the one having symptoms of some kind? Is it your partner? Is someone else in your family having difficultly functioning? Is it your son or daughter? Is someone acting out and getting into trouble? Do you feel things are out of control and about to explode? This is a good time to overcome your ambivalence and allow yourself to ask for help.

Communication

When asked, most couples requesting therapy point out that they need help with *communication* in their relationship. Frequently one partner will complain of not being heard and feeling very frustrated. The other partner will adamantly state that this is not the case, but he is just tired of the constant nagging and efforts to control. A decision is made at some point to "close one's ears" and stop listening. This becomes a way of holding onto power, independence, and dignity with a simple desire to be "left alone."

This can soon develop into a combative and passive-aggressive situation. "I'll take the garbage out when I want to, not when she wants me to!" he says.

"He doesn't listen," she says. This then becomes the way to complain about how others just don't do what is asked of them.

"He doesn't give me the respect I deserve or appreciate how hard I work," she says. He is labeled as "lazy" and she is considered a "bitch." This struggle is often perceived to be a *communication breakdown*.

Another form of communication breakdown happens when one partner has an expectation of the other partner but never shares it. Without knowing what's going on, the partner left in the dark may not have a clue and is left confused—a victim of senseless hurt and anger. Why is this senseless? It's because humans don't have the ability to read minds. So stop expecting the impossible from your partner! Try to communicate in a clear manner. Use words. Don't distort the communication process. Try to recognize what you want and, if it is reasonable, ask for it. Figure out *how* you can ask for it, *when* you can ask for it, and whether your partner will be in agreement.

If there is disagreement—and occasional disagreement between two people is normal and natural—talk about it. Try to better understand what is getting in the way and how it can be worked out. Some disagreements cannot be easily settled, even by using the best of conflict resolution skills. Are you able to go on living in the relationship by agreeing to disagree? Can you drop it for now? Is more time needed to process and evaluate what is being asked? Will life go on even if you don't get what you ask for? Will a growing resentment and hostility help your situation? Try to be more tolerant of your partner and have more faith in the strength of the relationship. If this is not possible, then it may be time to consider other alternatives.

Money

The next barrier worth discussing is *money*. The way money is managed within a family can make or break relationships. Who owns the money earned in your family? Do you own it because you earned it? Who spends the money? Are the bills paid before the money is spent on luxuries and recreation?

Who pays the bills? Do both of you know your expenses? Is there a budget and do you keep to it? Do you work up your credit cards living your life only for today, "maxed out" and in debt? Do you save anything for the kids' college fund or your own retirement? Do you have an emergency fund to buffer for a few months in case of a serious and unexpected situation? Who has access to the money? Do you keep your money separate, in two or more different accounts with your name only? When you look at money as a factor in your relationship, does it define a commitment to the both of you?

Marge and her husband John have two lovely daughters who are already grown and out of the house. Marge always left the money management to John and didn't think much about how she spent it. The girls always had the best of everything. She kept them and herself in the most fashionable of styles with clothing they enjoyed to the envy of their friends.

John quietly seethed by what he considered the spendthrift ways of his wife. He was tired of her lack of respect for a hard earned dollar. They weren't rich but she didn't pay attention to that fact and they paid the price of always having to catch up with bills—barely making it in their middle class lifestyle.

One day they decided to take a fancy vacation to the Mexican Riviera. While there, they were led into a sales talk for a timeshare. Prior to attending, they both firmly agreed that they would not buy in. They would simply listen to the sales pitch and leave the meeting with a $100 dinner certificate to a local seafood restaurant. That was the plan.

However, Marge was unable to keep her pact with John. The dream of having her own time-share in the sun was impossible for her to refuse. She would consider borrowing the money from her retirement savings, having worked ten years as a county employee.

Needless to say, Marge and John fought with each other at the sales meeting, and they fought all the way home. John just couldn't take it anymore. Their disagreement about money was a ticking time bomb that had now exploded. It was the last straw. Shortly after returning home, the couple separated. John moved out and they later divorced.

So, is it true what Joel Grey sings in the movie *Cabaret*? Does money really make "the world go 'round?" Or, is the pessimistic view about money being the "root of all evil" more accurate? I prefer to take the wiser view of my wife's dear uncle Bernie. He pointed out that money is merely a *vehicle* to get you where you want to go. However, in relationships it is important for a couple to have a shared value and understanding about the care and use of this vehicle. It can take you down a smooth road of convenience, comfort, and luxury. Or you can misuse it and drive yourself off the road entirely.

Commitment

Commitment to being physically present, such as nearby or in the same room or just generally more around and available, tends to crop up more frequently than expected in couple therapy sessions. I already spoke about emotional distancing or the shutting out of a partner by not listening or not responding to comments and questions. There are other ways to do this, as well: by spending all your time in another room, by always tinkering and fixing things in the garage, or by hiding out in the basement man cave.

Time and space are also taken away from the home by the *workaholic*. Working long hours often appears justified by the notion that one needs to bring home the bacon. However, if someone is working to excess, the partner left at home usually sees such an "excuse" for the cop-out that it is. It is an escape from participating in the family, not serving in the nurturing role as parent or spouse, and not proving loyalty to the emotional needs of the family system.

Unless some balance can be achieved between the responsibilities of work and home, family satisfaction can plummet for everyone. This can make family life very stressful and take the form of individual pathology. If this is happening to you, it may be helpful to take a hard look at yourself. Take an inventory to determine what is really important to you and your family. Does your family really need an absentee parent?

Sex

Sex is another important way of showing intimacy with your partner, though it can also sometimes evolve into a barrier in your relationship. When one or both of you are complaining that "we just don't get together that way anymore" or "it's just not enough," then it's time to take a closer look at this issue. Desire and satisfaction are important for sustaining the relationship and keeping the family intact.

Sometimes the problem that impairs sexual relations is a physical condition, and this might not always appear obvious. This is where consultation with a medical professional would be a good idea. Sometimes the problem may be a symptom of an underlying emotional issue, either with one person or with both. Regardless of the cause, your therapist can help you identify what's going on, and help move you and your partner in the direction of a healthier and happier sex life.

Infidelity

Infidelity becomes a suspicion when you are rarely home with your partner and kids. If they are jealous about all the time you spend away from home—allegedly because of work—can you imagine the feelings of abandonment, betrayal, and mistrust created by sneaking around and seeing another person?

But what if it is only a titillating computer activity such as an online relationship found on the internet? This appears to be an emerging problem seen more frequently in therapy sessions nowadays. It started off as just a simple form of curiosity and play, but it eventually took up more and more of your time and became an obsession.

Like an addiction to alcohol, drugs, gambling, or video games, infidelity pulls you away from your loved ones. It destroys the bonds that brought you together, and it is a sure way of seeing your family life crumble.

Addiction

Addiction is also a major cause of barriers to developing and maintaining intimacy with another person. It is a subject worthy of our attention because it affects not only the family but also our broader society. Issues of cover-up, *enabling*, and *codependency* all need to be addressed when someone is struggling with addiction. *Denial* needs to give way to recognition and acceptance.

There are many therapeutic resources in the community specializing in specific forms and stages of addiction. Medical care may be needed to assist with physical withdrawal. Rehabilitation services provide much needed education and direction to both the person with addiction and his or her family. Longer-term support may be recommended in the form of Alcoholic's Anonymous (AA) or Narcotics Anonymous (NA) meetings. *Recovery* is considered a lifelong process and many clients have shared the importance of "the rooms" as part of their therapeutic community to help prevent slips and relapses.

Let's Review

So far, we have gone over several barriers that can interfere with those you hold near and dear. These include communication, money, commitment, sex, infidelity, and addiction. In the next chapter we'll review even more barriers. You'll learn how selfishness, arrogance, ignorance, and stubbornness also interfere with the ability to achieve true intimacy. These are all quite closely connected to the barriers we already discussed.

Reviewing such barriers to intimacy may seem overwhelming. But don't get insulted and please don't give up! Take a breath of fresh air, take a break, and then keep on reading at your own pace. You know that you have the ability to make positive choices and become a mature, responsible, and loving person. Take my word for it, you can and will overcome these demons!

You may be thinking pessimistically, that "this is just too hard" and that you need to accept things exactly as they are. "It is what it is," you might say to yourself. But don't be resigned to inaction and passive hopelessness by these thoughts. You will recall that in previous chapters I discussed how your thoughts have almost everything to do with your emotions, your behavior, and the quality of your life. If you allow yourself to abandon this negative and self-defeating thinking, you'll be able to get back on track and start moving forward again. You can indeed achieve your goals! Stay the course and you can truly get what you want!

12

More Barriers
to Overcome

Parenting is one of the most important things you will ever do. It is also one of the most difficult of life tasks and there is no license or test to prove your readiness or competence. Some people have children for the wrong reasons. They think that a baby will save a flawed and soured relationship or perhaps make them feel more adult-like and whole. Others don't think about it and consider no consequences. They live their lives without planning, only to find their way into a surprise pregnancy and parenthood.

Of course, the better way is to prepare—to be emotionally, physically, and financially ready. Having a stable and loving home will increase the likelihood of a child growing into a healthy and productive adult. Learning right from wrong and functioning normally within our society requires the integration of appropriate values and independent living skills. Every stage of development introduces new challenges and encourages an educational process for both child and parents. The newborn needs to develop feelings of safety and trust to nourish and thrive. As a child grows, the environment should offer opportunities for exploration, discovery and self-confidence.

However, this process can also be hampered by an impoverished, neglectful, abusive, or over-restrictive environment, which holds back normal psychosocial development. An unstable home environment can lead to negative consequences when it comes to child rearing. Rather than the child feeling comfortable in his own skin, he may feel insecure, anxious, and uncertain about what is expected or how to behave. Emotional and behavioral problems emerge where the child begins to act out, have difficulty maturing or regress to a previous stage of development. For example, the toilet-trained toddler reverts back to being a baby and wets himself or the adolescent starts skipping school and repeatedly misses curfew. As I've already said, it's not easy having and raising children.

Developing a home environment conducive to healthy children requires parents to recognize the challenges, deal with the stressors as they come up and, most of all, work together as a team. If you are with spouse or partner, you may be lucky enough to have another adult to help in sharing extra work, engage in problem solving, and provide mutual support. This time can be very trying if your teenager is *splitting*, or playing one of you against the other. If you do not agree on appropriate expectations or consequences, and if both of you are not consistent with each other in your childrearing, then you are surely headed for serious trouble. When a child is out of control, resentment between parents may emerge and this will clearly become a barrier to any intimate relationship.

What if your child is in control but he or she presents with unexpected feelings and behaviors related to *gender identity* and *sexual orientation*? This too can become a challenge. Acceptance of the child unconditionally could be difficult for one or both of the parents and this may cause serious rifts to develop within the family. Life for all family members is affected. Dealing with the needs of the child, the parents and the family system as a whole can be further complicated by cultural stigma attached to this situation. But it is helpful to note that society is in the midst of change. Alternative lifestyles are becoming more commonplace and accepted in many communities.

Religious and cultural values may also come into play, causing a divide between partners and an end to what once was a loving relationship. Ira and Joan had to face this barrier and it became a painful challenge that they were unable to overcome. They met in college and soon fell madly in love. Right after graduation they married and both worked in professional careers. Ira's background was Jewish. His grandparents were from Eastern Europe. They fled to America to avoid persecution and to survive the Holocaust. His parents assimilated well in this country but they insisted he have a Jewish education early in life and a bar mitzvah when he was thirteen.

Joan, on the other hand, was born and raised as a Catholic. Her family had a head start in America, having come from the Netherlands many generations ago. When the couple noted their differences early in their relationship, they stuck by a liberal point of view and considered their love for each other the overriding factor, the one force that would see them through any conflict and sustain their bond.

However, three years into the marriage, they started talking about having children. How would these children be raised? What religion would they be? This became more and more of a problem with each holding the position of their own upbringing and with each having strong feelings about passing on a pure rather than hybrid heritage. By Christmas of their fourth year together, Ira would have no tree or decorations in *his* home. Naturally, Joan balked by this unilateral decision and firmly held her ground. However, there was no resolution to this dilemma and love did not ride out the storm. Their marriage did not last through the fifth year. Ira moved out, and separation led to divorce. They never kept a friendship. Both moved to different cities and tried to pick up the pieces of their lives after the breakup.

Sometimes a breakup is the best decision for all concerned, and for Ira and Joan this may have been the best solution. But depending on your unique situation, it is possible to weather the stormy challenges of a long-term intimate relationship. In the next chapter, I'll introduce you to some helpful hints.

13

The ABC's of Successful Marriage

Choosing a partner is a life-altering decision. The bond with your spouse better be a strong one if you willingly agreed to the oath "'til death do us part." This phase of life is a transition from the connective bond with parents to a new role of interdependence and cooperation with another person. The two of you are indeed significant to each other and should be supportive. You have decided to become a team. Together you will approach, enter, and deal with whatever comes your way while carving out a life with each other and making your own nuclear family. This life phase will require a new level of maturity. You will need to start thinking about "We" rather than "Me." Now, don't get frightened by this! If you both do your part, the team inevitably wins and you both share in the glory and satisfaction of the success.

The *ABC's of marriage* or successful partnership presented here is not the same as the ABC Model of REBT that was introduced in chapter 8. The ABC Model of REBT was an *individual* model of cognition, to help you identify and change your thoughts. The ABC's of marriage is more of an *interper-*

sonal model, designed to help you to remember some very important ideas that are necessary to keep your intimacy and marriage alive.

The A's of Marriage

What are the A's? Think of the following list and what it means to you: *admiration, adulation, affection, acknowledgment, appreciation, affirmation, approval, acceptance, availability, awareness, accommodation,* and *agreement.* You are welcome to add other A words that apply, but this is a good start and ought to do it for now. These A words are behaviors that are surely in your best interest in developing and keeping a bond with your mate. They are the ingredients of a loving attitude that will hold you both together over a lifetime.

A young mother came in to see me feeling depressed about her marriage. She loved her husband and wanted him to love her back but she felt neglected and abandoned. He worked on the railroad crew fixing tracks and maintaining equipment. His job took him away from home for days and sometimes weeks at a time. She wanted him to join her in therapy but he had no interest in participating. She did not have the marriage she wanted and felt stressed by the thought of him leaving for the next job away from home. This unwelcome anticipation was always there, like a constant heavy weight upon her.

However, she was dedicated to keeping her marriage intact and as happy as possible. She was raised in a broken family and didn't want the same for her own child. In therapy, she began to realize that the more she nagged her husband about his job, the more she was pushing him away. She started to address her depression and dependency in the sessions. As a result, she began to expand her own interests and contacts, which she did by volunteering with a local social service agency. She also became more willing to spend time with friends and family. She focused more attention on her son's schedule, finding opportunities to enrich his education and social growth.

She vowed to make the limited time with her husband more meaningful and enjoyable. As she became less needy and demanding, time at home became more pleasant for her husband. He, in turn, felt more accepted and empowered as the family provider and breadwinner. He began to spend more time at home with the family and even considered ways of changing his work schedule.

Sometimes life circumstances get in the way of marital stability and satisfaction. It becomes difficult to apply what is really needed to make things work. Keep in mind that you only have control over yourself! Bitching, moaning, whining, nagging and complaining about what the other person does or does not do, only leads to the opposite result. No one wants to feel that they are being controlled and they will stubbornly refuse to change. They will fight back to maintain their ground.

What is the best way to help another person change within a relationship? Look at what *you* need to do to change. This means doing some self-analysis, developing a realistic plan and acting on it. Part of your plan is to be patient about the outcome and realize that it may take some time to see success. After all, Rome wasn't built in a day!

The B's of Marriage

What are the B's? They are: *believing* in the *beauty* of your relationship and what it has to offer. There is nothing wrong with having love, companionship, stability, satisfaction, and joy. You deserve to have these, and they are your right.

By having a solid *bond* with your partner, you can achieve what is truly important. You will come to see that the whole is in fact much greater than the sum of its parts. You may also come to realistically see that perfection is only a myth, and the future of any relationship is clearly the responsibility of both partners.

The C's of Marriage

Finally, we come to the C's. Try these on for size: *commitment, connection, communication, consideration, cooperation, compromise, courtesy,* and *compassion.* Yes, you are fully capable of making good things happen within a *caring* relationship, especially if you don't let your selfish needs interfere too much. There is hope because C also stands for *choice,* and it's yours to make as much as your partner's.

Think about how to apply these ideas to your own marriage. They can work by making your marriage stronger or saving it from falling apart. Don't let *complacency* set in. Take responsibility and not be *culpable* by allowing the marriage to take a dive. These last two C's may lead to the big D—divorce.

While divorce is not the end of the world, it is not likely what you signed up for or what you expected. It is one of those unfortunate outcomes leading to numerous hassles and inconveniences, especially if there are children involved. For some people who are just not able to get past themselves, it may be the least painful alternative.

On the more positive side, divorce is an opportunity to start anew—to make necessary changes and rebuild a more satisfying future—perhaps even find a new partner. You can then try the ABC's once again.

Part IV

—

Overcoming Life Challenges

14

Childhood Trauma: Abuse, Neglect, & Abandonment

My father would come home drunk, beat my mother and then turn on me. I learned to fight back and finally got out at the age of 16.

—F.K.

My mother was addicted to crack. She took in a lot of guys and there were times when she was gone for days at a time. We went to live with my grandmother until she died of a stroke.

—G.M.

I never told anyone about this, but I was molested by my cousin at an early age.

—J.R.

I was always criticized by my father. It seemed there was nothing I could do right. Then the bullying came in school. I think they all knew I was gay, even before I came out.

—E.J.

What happens to people exposed to an environment of chaos, abuse, neglect, and abandonment? How do they feel about themselves and the world around them? These are important questions to ask for an understanding of the feelings and motivations of many unfortunate souls who, by no fault of their own, happen to be born and reared by irresponsible parents. As you would expect, many of these individuals are damaged in the process and suffer with poor self-esteem, depression, mistrust and anger at the uncertainty of the world. Many have difficulty forming and maintaining stable relationships. Completing school, keeping a job, and contributing positively to society may be interrupted by this damage. It is not uncommon for these victims of childhood to make poor life choices, losing years of their lives to substance abuse, legal problems, chronic medical illnesses, or homelessness.

Glen R. Shiraldi (2001) writes vividly and perceptively about how "abuse, abandonment, criticism, and/or neglect interact with personal fallibilities and choices. They lead people to conclude that they are defective and flawed as individuals. They don't believe that they *make* mistakes; but instead that they *are* a mistake, bad at the core."

All is not lost, however. On the positive side, it is good to know that humans are incredibly resilient. I've said it before and I'll say it again. We can all heal and become the person we want to be, and yes, this means you! There are just a few things that you need to understand: *self-esteem*, *shame*, and *inner child*. Knowing about these will help you get started in the healing process on your way toward a healthier self.

Just what exactly is *self-esteem* and how do you get it? Well, we know that it is not something physical, like blue eyes or blonde hair. There are lots of good-looking people who are not happy with their self-image and suffer from low self-esteem. However, it is something you usually can see in a person who displays confidence and dignity.

Again, Shiraldi helps us in definition: "It's preferable to say simply that people possess self-esteem when they have a realistic and appreciative opinion of themselves." This means being able to like who you are, and feel good about yourself, despite the recognition that you will never be perfect. It may be more accurate to say that self-esteem is a form of *self-acceptance*. You can take all of your human traits, acknowledge the good with the bad, and still keep a favorable appraisal of yourself. This can be very hard to do, especially if you have been living with a negative pattern of self-deprecating thoughts and self-sabotaging behaviors for many years.

Shame, another factor to face and overcome, is an overpowering emotion from a painful past. It relentlessly lingers and makes you suffer with horribly low self-esteem. It encompasses a strong feeling of humiliation and self-blame. It overshadows feelings of guilt and regret by its very nature—its overwhelming threat to one's core being, and its fear of discovery. It is based on the idea that one has done wrong, even if that's not an objective reality. Nevertheless, it is considered by the individual as dishonorable, immoral, and in violation of social norms.

For example, a child physically or sexually victimized may experience harmful shame far into adulthood. The perception of having done wrong or being wrong may also feed the shame of an individual unable to reach an expected standard or state of being. For example, a person who is gay or overweight may suffer this painful emotion as a consequence of social disapproval and severe criticism.

Shame, can also be the result of a close association with

the disturbing acts of others, such as family members. All too often, the children of alcoholic parents experience this emotion. It is like poison that prevents you from trusting. It keeps you in hiding, not allowing others in, not letting them know what you have endured, not sharing how you really feel about yourself and how you really feel about the world around you. It is a destructive force, a barrier in therapy, and something you must address to get well. That means taking the risk of seriously talking about this pain. You have the task of trusting your therapist enough to explain how it came about and how you continue to keep it going, despite your best efforts otherwise.

John Bradshaw (1988) spoke about finding ways to heal the "shame that binds you." He likened it to a form of "internal bleeding" and considered it to be "toxic" and "excruciating because it is the painful exposure of the believed failure of self to the self." He explained that it is experienced as, "the all-pervasive sense that I am flawed and defective as a human being." He further clarified that "*toxic shame* is the feeling of being isolated and alone in a complete sense. A shame-based person is haunted by a sense of absence and emptiness."

Almost all of my clients who suffered from horribly low self-esteem and shame gave a history of some form of severe trauma in childhood. Somehow, it seemed to make an indelible mark on their lives. They carried around a hurt and wounded *inner child*. The school of psychology called *transactional analysis* advanced by authors Eric Berne and Thomas Harris, spoke about the "child" within and the repeated patterns of interaction that comprised a person's *life script*. When this script is negative, the child feels "not okay" and takes on the attitude, emotions and behavior consistent with that position. Harris (1969) wrote, "The script may call for a life of withdrawal, since it is too painful to be around okay people." He went on to write, "Another person's script may call for behavior which is provoking to the point where others turn on him (*nega-*

tive stroking), thus proving once again, 'I'm not okay.' This is the case of the *bad little boy*. 'You say I'm bad so I'll be bad!' He may kick and spit and claw his way through life and thus achieve a fraudulent integrity with at least one constant he can count on: 'I'm not ok—You're ok.' There is a kind of miserable sense in this, in that the integrity of the position is maintained, but it leads to despair."

Many of the clients I have worked with in therapy wished that they were treated differently in childhood. It would have helped them to feel "okay" and make a better adjustment to the world. However, they continued to struggle with the reality of damaged parents and the experience of an unhealthy upbringing. Their formative years were insecure and undesirable. For them, these years may be described as an emotional and physical battle to survive. Their later years continued to reflect this battle.

Some may not have experienced the wounds of childhood from their parental home. Instead, they found themselves in a hostile environment as they entered school and dealt with peers. For one reason or another, they did not have the tools to deal with the competitive nature of this peer interaction and were victims of harsh criticism, exclusion and bullying. They were vulnerable and therefore viciously attacked by the other kids. One client told me, "It was like I was carrying around a sign on my forehead." He was indeed fragile and ill prepared for the insensitivity and abuse by the other kids. He was also confused that the environment was not safer and more protective. The same could also be true in the neighborhood streets or parks where groups of kids gather with little or no responsible supervision.

How do we take care of the hurting inner child? First, it is important to know that this child is a free-spirited, fun-loving, curious, rebellious, and enjoyable kid. You need to believe that this child is really worthy of your care and attention. You may have expected something very different from those who disappointed you in those earlier years. But, no matter how much you hoped for otherwise, you were left with the unpleasant reality of what occurred.

One person said, "If they would only apologize to me, say they were sorry, then I would be able to turn things around and make more of a life for myself." To have that wish fulfilled would be very nice, but it's not advisable to set yourself up in this way! It will likely result in even more distress.

Today, you are the one who needs to take positive action! Why? Because you are now an adult and you have acquired knowledge and wisdom. Now is the time for you to be that loving and comforting guardian who will rescue this hurting inner child from the past.

Imagine this "little one" standing at the door of your childhood home. What does this little girl or little boy look like? Is she a small version of you? Take her hand in yours and softly tell her not to be afraid. You are there to protect her and care for her. As long as she is with you, she will never be hurt again. Tell her to come along and walk with you hand in hand into the future. This is a future of safety and love. It is a time of nurturing and hope.

It is not easy to undo the damage of childhood trauma. Embracing the ideas offered in this book and learning to move forward takes some courage. I know that you want to get beyond your disturbing past. You are tired of feeling down and unworthy. Perhaps these feelings are all too familiar.

But to get better you've got to start somewhere, and so perhaps now is the time to feel okay and truly be okay. Ask yourself the following questions: Can you let go of the past and leave it there? Can you get to a place of acceptance and forgiveness? Can you free yourself of the anger and torment? Can you, in essence, move on?

Working with your therapist will help you to learn how

to dispel the distortions in your thinking and improve your self-esteem. Reflecting on your past pain and restructuring your present view will be a collaborative effort.

Therapy is not a magic pill, and won't work overnight. But if you stay with it and have faith in the process, you will get better. Remember that you are safe and no one will hurt you. Your healing will come and you will become a stronger person, feeling more whole and better about yourself.

15

I Can't Help Myself

We've all heard the Nike commercial with the encouragement to "Just do it!" The assumption, of course, is that the result will be a positive and rewarding one. However, we cannot take this advice carte blanche. Not all results work out for the better and there should be some realistic thought about outcome before an action is taken. Problems may arise when the thought process is too quick and weak. The same is true when one thinks too much and is driven by strong unwelcome false ideas. In this chapter, I will begin to describe two problem categories that share the same behavioral spectrum but fall on opposite sides of the continuum. These are problems related to *impulsivity* and *compulsivity*.

While these two categories of behavior are usually addressed separately, they do appear to be cousins by their similarities. Both are experienced as a subjective urge or impulse to *act out* in a particular way. The need to *let go* usually wins out over the more acceptable behavior of holding back. Lack of control or self-restraint is an issue in both cases.

With impulsivity, the reward factor is usually viewed as

overwhelmingly strong and seemingly impossible to resist. The behavioral release is based on the fulfillment of some perceived pleasure. If there is a negative consequence, and there usually is, this is often overlooked. The person suffering from impulsivity will experience a sense of arousal or tension just prior to doing it, and a feeling of empowerment, achievement, and gratification at the time of performing the act. At some level, they may be aware that what they are doing is wrong, socially inappropriate, or even illegal, but the positive feeling and pleasure derived from the act is just too great and not easily thwarted. In short, this person is saying to himself, "It feels really good and I don't care about anything else right now." It's like having a high feeling and going with it to enjoy the ride. This person may later regret his behavior but tends to have a short memory for any negative consequences.

The person suffering from compulsivity, on the other hand, also acts out but this is because of feeling compelled to do so. The behavior is initially felt as an impulse, thought, idea or image that is unwanted and recognized by the person as unacceptable. This is known as an *obsession*. This obsession is accompanied by an overwhelming tension or anxiety that is immediately relieved as a result of the act. In this situation, the person is saying to himself: "It feels really bad if I don't do anything," and "I do care." When a person experiences this pattern of thought and behavior, they sometimes receive the diagnosis of *obsessive-compulsive disorder* (OCD).

While the person with impulsivity seems to be motivated by some form of perceived *positive reinforcement* (a reward of some kind), the person with compulsivity seems to be motivated by a perceived *negative reinforcement* (avoidance of emotional distress). In either case, whether you are impulsive or compulsive, there appears to be a *build up* and a *letting go* process. Good judgment with attention to consequences gives way to problem behavior. The decision seems automatic and outside of conscious awareness. The person comes into a therapist's office and usually says, "I can't help myself."

One example of an *impulse control disorder* is *pathological gambling*. Because of the habit forming and persistent nature of this difficulty, you might also think of this as an addiction, a term usually reserved for people suffering from overuse of substances and having a strong physiological component. Nevertheless, I've seen numerous clients with this problem in my practice and I have seen them struggle. They frequently came into therapy after realizing that their uncontrolled behavior was an incredible burden to their family as well as their wallets. Spouses threatened to leave them and take the children if they didn't do something quickly to get help. Thousands of dollars have been lost and squandered by these clients. All because of the fantasy of "winning big" and chasing their losses. I have seen clients face serious legal problems with years of imprisonment after embezzling money to feed their frenzy to gamble.

Impulsivity is a trait also seen with many other mental health conditions. For example, a person suffering with *attention deficit disorder, bipolar disorder*, or a *personality disorder* will experience difficulties with self-restraint. While each mental health condition has its own definition and parameters, when impulsivity is involved you can expect there will be trouble.

When compulsivity rears it's ugly head, it too causes pain. Larry was a fifty-year-old, married man, who held a responsible professional position in the community. He came into therapy with the complaint that his ritual checking behavior was "getting in the way." It was causing him to be late for work. His boss had taken notice and he knew that something had to be done. Every day, while backing out of his driveway, he would hit the garage door remote in his car and then drive away. However, as he got halfway to work, he would question whether the door went down and stayed down. Anxiety about the garage door open all day and the house being robbed was just too much for him to bear. He would turn the car around and drive back home to check. What a relief he felt when he confirmed that the door was indeed closed. However, this checking behavior became a daily drudgery. This is a good example of how compulsivity gets in the way of normal functioning.

Sigmund Freud, the father of *psychoanalysis*, spoke of impulsivity and compulsivity as having their origins in human biology and appearing in the earliest years of life. At birth, we are instinctively driven by unbridled impulses in the absence of language and moral understanding. Infants expect comforts and pleasures to come with immediate gratification. The cry of an infant in need of a diaper change or hungry for a nipple is a clear simple image and proof of these ideas. As the infant becomes a toddler, he or she begins to learn more about right from wrong through mother's loving guidance.

But there is still a long way to go for the personality to develop and the child to become fully socialized. Around the age of two, children begin to assert their independence by resisting adult authority with the very word they've heard over and over again: "No." We have come to identify this phase as the terrible two's. Another battle emerges at this time over toilet training. As the anal sphincter develops, the child can be in a position of power over the parent. The child is developing physical control to either "hold onto" or "let go" of bodily waste. The decision becomes voluntary, and is connected with the quality of the parental relationship and satisfaction of needs. Toilet training can become a messy battle. It is this aspect of the anal phase of development that has been likened to the dilemma of the compulsive adult. Freudian analysis will consider the obsessive-compulsive problem to have its roots in this stage of development.

In addition to presenting various phases of psychological development, Freud went on to explain the theoretical structure and process of the mind by discussing how drives and impulses of the pleasure-seeking *id* are balanced by the moral conscience of the *superego* and the rationality of the *ego*. When things go awry and these processes are overwhelmed, ego *defense mechanisms* come into play or *neuroses* will develop.

While all this may sound rather obtuse, it did give some theoretical framework for psychodynamic therapists. It gave credence to the psychological and developmental roots associated with emotional and behavioral problems. It gave further explanation and understanding of impulsivity and compulsivity in the human psyche.

Now, let's turn our attention to the treatment of these problems. Your therapist, if psychoanalytically trained, may spend much time on developing a dynamic understanding of your childhood. Interpretations and insights could be helpful. Working through childhood conflicts within the therapeutic relationship by *transference* may also be very helpful. This is when the client feels and acts toward the therapist as if he were a significant figure from the past, such as a parent. However, based on my own experience and knowledge, I prefer a more direct and practical approach using cognitive-behavioral and biological methods.

For people struggling with either an impulse control problem or extreme compulsivity, their first goal is to acknowledge that their repeated "giving in" to the urge, temptation, or drive will usually come with a harmful negative consequence, and this needs to stop. With insight one learns more about the origins of their behavior. It is also through insight that one recognizes the connection between their own behavior and its outcome. This is called *consequential thinking* and it works best when it is intact at the moment of decision-making. The impulsive person also needs to identify their *high-risk situations* and initially avoid them. So, if you stop off at the local coffee shop on your way to work and happen to get tempted by the Lotto and Powerball displays, take another route and don't stop there! Get your coffee at another shop that doesn't sell the Quick Picks!

The next thing you will be doing with your cognitive-behavioral therapist is looking at your erroneous thinking connected to your destructive impulsive behavior. Some thoughts may be as follows: "This time is different because I have a strong feeling about these numbers; That slot machine hasn't hit in awhile, and it's due; or I'm carrying my lucky key-chain." Yes, you may have a knack for convincing yourself that it's okay to "give in" to your impulse. You may also have an excuse for losing or you rationalized it as a "price to pay" while waiting for your "big win."

But when you stop, take the time to look at the disappointment on your spouse's face, think about your total losses and attend to reality, you will recognize that the only real winner here is the lottery commission, racing establishment, or casino. The focus of your therapy is to look at yourself, dig deep to identify the erroneous thoughts or magical ideas specific to you. You'll need to use your mental power to think more rationally—to vigorously work at challenging those crazy thoughts or ideas that cause you to "give in" to your negative impulses. This is a process called *cognitive restructuring*. The result will be replacing those irrational ideas with more rational thoughts and replacing your self-defeating actions with more appropriate behaviors.

Now, you may initially believe that you have no control at all over your thoughts or behaviors. This is not true! The element of *choice* is a strong factor here and you do in fact have it! So, what are you going to do about it? Help is certainly out there and you can work with a qualified therapist to take back your life. I'm sure your family and friends would be fully behind you with that decision. But don't expect the therapist to do it all for you. A therapist will guide you along the way but the work is for you to do. For whatever it's worth, I'm also in your court. I think you can do it. So, go ahead!

Bruce Hyman and Cherry Pedrick (1999) do a very nice job of explaining and outlining effective treatment strategies in *The OCD Workbook, Your Guide to Breaking Free from Obsessive Compulsive Disorder.* They point out that this program can be self-directed and that preparation means setting a clear and significant amount of time aside to work on it, while making it the "most important priority in your life." It is important that you have informed your family for their support and that you have a knowledgeable coach or therapist on board to help you stay focused and to tackle the difficult tasks. They discuss an *anxiety exposure list* used for gradual *exposure and ritual prevention* (ERP). "In exposure and ritual prevention, blocking rituals with ritual prevention reduces obsessive worries by means of extinction. By blocking behaviors that reinforce worries and keep them going, obsessional worries eventually diminish." In this therapeutic procedure, the person suffering with obsessive-compulsive behaviors gradually exposes himself to triggering stimuli or situations. He then allows himself to tolerate the expected discomfort without performing the ritualistic behaviors.

ERP can be very difficult to do and this is why a supportive and firm partner may be just what you need to get through it. It is entirely possible to withhold, not give in to the urge and, in turn, develop much improved tolerance. This may seem counterintuitive because you are now following a more rational and behavioral approach rather than your immediate gut feelings. Although it is distressing to initially go through this process, you need to tell yourself and be convinced that you will be okay. Saying that it is "too hard" will keep you stuck with your OCD. So remember: Your goal is to overcome this dysfunction.

Let me add a few words here about medication. There is nothing wrong with seeing a doctor to obtain medication for help with these problems. It may take the edge off and help you to move along more comfortably. More often than not, it is the combined approach of medication with cognitive behavioral therapy or REBT that is the most helpful. When you use medication, make sure that you are seeing someone who is an expert with these medications and make sure that you tell your therapist who you are seeing and what you are taking. Collaboration and communication are important for the best results. Everyone, including you, is part of the team whose goal is to see you get better.

16

Anxiety and Panic

When anxiety and panic set in, you become frozen and immobilized. Everything appears to stop or slow down, where life seems surreal and perhaps distant. Concentration is lost and you are unable to think or maintain focus. Think of the deer in the road that just stays there, staring at the lights of the upcoming automobile. Think of yourself trying to read a book or answer a question on an exam. You are pressured to read the same sentence over and over again without a grasp of the meaning. You are unable to process information accurately. Your muscles are tense, your stomach is in a knot, and your thoughts are jumbled and foggy. You feel unable to function and broken, which further worries and upsets you. You feel restless, on edge, and have difficulty sleeping. You may also be irritable and fatigued, not your usual self. When this is an experience that plagues you almost all of the time, it's called *generalized anxiety disorder.*

A *panic attack* is different from the generalized feeling of apprehension and nervousness one experiences with chronic anxiety. Panic is an acute event with sudden onset of intense terror accompanied by such symptoms as shortness of breath, sweating, dizziness, trembling, heart palpitations, and fear of dying, "going crazy" or losing control.

Panic attacks may occur out of the blue in places one might consider to be *triggers* for future attacks. Some of these places may be the grocery store, driving a car, taking a bus, or using an elevator. When these places are identified and associated by the panic-ridden person, an avoidance pattern may occur. If this avoidance sets in, the anxiety becomes even more debilitating because the person starts to cut him- or herself off from the rest of the world. This is known as *agoraphobia*. It is wise to get help before you get to this point. The earlier you deal with this problem, the better chance you'll have of beating it.

Of course, you have probably heard of other irrational fears or *phobias*. These include a fear of heights (*acrophobia*), small spaces (*claustrophobia*), germs or contamination (*mysophobia*), animals (*zoophobia*), foreigners or strangers (*xenophobia*), and losing a job (*ergophobia*). The list of phobias goes on and on. Again, if you are having irrational fears, anxiety and panic that interfere with the quality of your life, it might be time to find a therapist to help you.

Ned entered therapy wondering how he would stay in his job. He was afraid that he would have to quit or get fired, stay home, and never come out. He worked at a local delicatessen and actually loved making sandwiches for customers. He proudly spoke of himself as an "artist" and considered every sandwich he made a unique work of art. However, his anxiety was getting the best of him. He was given the responsibility of closing the shop and this came with several tasks, all of which had to be done by day's end.

As the closing hour came closer, he became less able to function. He felt numb and confused. He reported, "I'd be sweating, shaking, and have a heaviness in my chest." He wasn't sure whether he could complete all the tasks necessary by closing time. He wasn't sure whether he could actually get out and be ready to go home on time. Ned was overwhelmed by his *what if thinking* and exaggerated expectations of himself. What if he forgot to do something? What if he was late? When we tackled these questions, we looked at the worst possible outcomes and the likelihood of these actually occurring. If he forgot a step, would it truly result in the loss of his job? If he were to need more time and get home later, would it be the end of the world? If he could not measure up exactly every time, would his ego be crushed?

Ned was helped to make a checklist of the steps he needed to take for closing. This way he would be assured of not missing anything before leaving the shop. He lived alone and usually had no particular plans immediately after work. Getting home a little later would not be more than a mere inconvenience, if that.

By focusing on his job as the activating event, we were able to look more closely into Ned's deeper thoughts at the root of his problem. Ned was afraid of failure and wanted to have complete control over his situation. As he would later come to see, his thinking was unrealistic and led to his anxiety. Not all consequences are catastrophic and not all situations can be in his complete control. As he adjusted his thinking, Ned approached work in a much calmer manner. He also learned deep abdominal breathing, which he frequently used to manage anxious feelings. To his surprise, he became a valued employee, recognized for his efforts and offered an opportunity for a position in management.

Some people who suffer from anxiety are not able to fully resolve their symptoms by just talking about their issues and confronting their conflicts. They tend to be anxious-prone by nature, hypersensitive to symptoms of anxiety, and in need of more immediate relief. These individuals are quite vulnerable, and they find themselves feeling anxious about becoming anxious. This *secondary anxiety* becomes a problem quite difficult to get beyond. For those who are this sensitive, the use of medication can be very helpful. Anti-anxiety medication along with cognitive behavioral therapy are effective in sequence and combination. Exercises for self-calming and *relaxation* taught and used properly can also work wonders. Once the symptoms are better managed, these anxiety sufferers are more amenable to work on battling distorted thinking and confronting target situations.

Just what exactly is *anxiety*? To answer this question, it is first important to understand the difference between anxiety and *fear*. They both have the same physiological components, so how are they different? The psychologist, Paul Hauck (1975), gives an excellent explanation by "choosing to define a fear specifically and only as a feeling of threat from a cause of which you are aware, and anxiety as a feeling of threat from a cause of which you are not aware." More simply said, "When you do not know what you are afraid of, you are experiencing anxiety." Clients who understand this difference become more capable of working on their anxiety. Awareness of your fears gives greater definition to the problem and improves your grasp on it. It makes way for further therapeutic work and offers the hope of an eventual freedom from suffering.

There are also a number of physiological effects that occur when you are experiencing anxiety, fear or panic. These combined effects have been more commonly referred to in the scientific community as the *fight or flight reaction*. When perceiving a threat, whether it is physical or psychological, the body reacts by activating the *sympathetic nervous system* to create hyper-arousal. *Adrenaline* and *cortisol* are released into the bloodstream, the heart pumps harder, breathing becomes more rapid, and muscles tighten. The end result is feeling tense, stressed, uncomfortable, and quite nervous.

It is important for you to understand that having anxiety

and panic does not mean that you are sentenced to death, permanent loss of control, craziness, or a life in an institution. Yes, it is an uncomfortable experience, but thinking these things makes it that much worse than it actually is. There is no evidence that these ideas are true. I have never known anyone to have these things happen as a result of anxiety or panic. Have you? How long have you been having symptoms? Are you still around? You are here, free, not crazy, living, breathing, and reading this book.

The more you learn about anxiety, the less you will be afraid of it and the less likely you will be of getting yourself into a full blown panic attack. You will come to realize that it is nothing more than a state of physiological discomfort that comes and goes. It will pass and you will eventually become more accepting of this fact, better tolerate it, and not add further thoughts of horror about having it. This is how it escalates for sure and becomes an overwhelming condition. When you recognize that you can get through it without building it way out of proportion, you will then find the anxiety to lessen over time. Your episodes will become less frequent and less intense.

So, how can you reduce your anxiety? I'd like to share with you some cognitive-behavioral exercises and other helpful hints to better manage the onset of anxiety symptoms and to prevent their recurrence. It means doing something much different than you usually do to improve or overcome this problem. Cognitive-behavioral exercises will help you to reduce the undesirable feelings you have with anxiety. They will also switch on the *parasympathetic nervous system*, which comes to the rescue to reduce the physiological effects. You will then turn down the hyper-arousal in favor of calm, restful, and peaceful feelings.

Using these exercises and making some changes are important steps in helping you reduce the anxiety. Keep in mind that the more you work on it, the better you will become. It will get easier and faster over time for you to feel better. So, don't give up! Discuss this further with your therapist to clarify instructions and to answer any questions.

You can learn more about cognitive-behavioral exercises at WilliamLKnupp.com, but here's an overview of some that can prove helpful for your anxiety, along with other interventions, as well. I encourage you to try one or more of the following suggestions and see how they work for you.

Deep Breathing

Paying attention to your breath as a life anchor while using it as a tool to improve the exchange of oxygen and carbon dioxide in your body will help reduce anxiety and bring on a greater sense of well-being. *Deep breathing* is a simple way to turn on an immediate relaxation response. The beauty of it is that you can use it almost anywhere with no special need for equipment. Deep breathing has also been shown to have positive long-term health benefits and this certainly is a bonus.

Progressive Muscle Relaxation

This exercise brings attention to your muscles. It requires that you alternate the tightening and loosening of major muscle groups to induce muscle relaxation throughout your body. It is usually combined with a form of deep breathing. The therapist provides instructional patter and redirects attention to the muscles feeling lighter, heavier or warmer.

Progressive muscle relaxation is usually performed in a reclining position with eyes closed, shoes off, and clothes loosened. It takes 15 to 20 minutes per session and is recommended twice per day over a prolonged period of 4 to 6 weeks. It is a deliberate effort to learn how to achieve a relaxation response and to more naturally re-experience this state through the magic of muscle memory. An audiotape can be made with your therapist or one can be readily purchased in most bookstores.

Meditation & Mindfulness

Both meditation and mindfulness became more popular in mid-20th century America and have received increasing scientific credibility for their benefits with health, mental health, and general well-being.

Meditation involves a shift of concentration inward to clear the mind of active everyday thought, achieving a calm and quiet state. In Transcendental Meditation a *mantra* is used, which is a word or sound helpful to the process of blocking unwanted thoughts and clearing the mind.

Mindfulness is also a purposeful redirection of attention and conscious awareness to the present moment. The experience is nonjudgmental where any extraneous and interfering thoughts, feelings or sensations are merely noted and fully accepted. An experienced and certified instructor is recommended for both of the above.

Imagery

It is the use of the mind's eye that defines the *imagery* experience, requiring you to visualize a relaxing or serene scene. It can be used to improve specific skills, such as imagining your ability to overcome a public speaking anxiety, or more broadly for the purpose of feeling safe and having an increased sense of well-being.

During an imagery exercise, you are instructed to close your eyes and try to see a calm picture in your mind or think deeply about successfully performing an activity or being in a favorite comfortable space. Imagery can also be used as an adjunct to relaxation exercises. For example, you may be asked to think of your stress as an inflated balloon while imagining it float away.

A client of mine, Joseph, used imagery to help cope with his fear of flying. He was afraid of the bouncing motions from the air turbulence during commercial flights. He closed his eyes and reminded himself of a vacation happily floating on the water of a Caribbean beach. The bouncing of the waves, slight warm breeze, and beautiful scenery of sand and palm trees filled his mind. It helped him to feel much calmer and dispense with his growing fears.

Self-Persuasion

Convincing yourself to take a rational view when you're feeling anxious is no easy task but can be very powerful. *Self-persuasion* requires combatting your *what if thinking* and pushing yourself to acknowledge that the worst possible scenario is truly a rarity.

Donald Meichenbaum (1972, 1985) developed a successful treatment approach called *stress inoculation training* (SIT), a form of self-persuasion. It uses education, skill acquisition and rehearsal to help a person deal with stressful events before, during, and after their occurrence. Through use of various therapeutic techniques including cognitive restructuring, self-instruction, coping statements, and positive reinforcement (self-praise), events once expected to trigger anxiety are successfully managed in stages. Over the years, this approach has been expanded by the addition of such exercises as relaxation and imagery. SIT has been applied to several different populations encountering a variety of problems, including pain management, anger, trauma, and athletic performance.

Kevin took a family vacation to Ireland where he was expected to climb the steep and narrow steps of Blarney Castle to perform the traditional kissing of the Blarney Stone. Although he wanted to do this and saw many people safely making the climb, his body was telling him otherwise. He felt anxious with butterflies in his stomach, wobbly knees, and weakness in his legs. He was going downhill fast! He knew it would be difficult but promptly told himself that he came over 3,000 miles for this experience and would not miss the opportunity. He asked his wife for support and she willingly became an encouraging lieutenant in this *in vivo exposure*.

He knew that he would have to face and tolerate a great deal of distress, but the outcome would be a huge success. It made his travels much more pleasurable and enriching. Kevin used several stress inoculation techniques to deal with his situation. He kept in a problem-solving frame of mind, and accepted his anxiety while confronting the stressor. He then persuaded himself to continue climbing the steps by using self-talk to remain rational, and provide self-instruction to positively cope with his situation. His reward was in the successful completion of the activity while overcoming his fears. And when Kevin successfully completed the climb, he also saw the value of self-praise for getting through it.

Living a Healthy Lifestyle

Eating and drinking right while getting good sleep and exercise is just what the doctor ordered. We all know that good health is a prescription for better tolerating stress. If you frequently feel hyper-aroused or anxious, why would you consume caffeine? If you have difficulties with impulsivity, anger, or emotional regulation, why would you drink alcohol or use street drugs?

Living a *healthy lifestyle* is about making the right choices and not accepting excuses, including any claim that these matters are out of your control. But at the same time, don't give yourself a guilt trip if you fall off track! None of us are perfect. However, you know that you can make healthier choices and it would be better to put more effort into this. Why not get the natural feeling of well-being from the endorphins released during vigorous exercise? Why not tone up and improve your endurance? And while we're on the subject of health, why not make a real commitment to give up those cigarettes?

Yoga

Yoga is a practice dating back to ancient India where Hindu and Buddhist monks considered it as a discipline to integrate the mind, body, and spirit. In present day Western culture, it is practiced as a physical exercise using various poses and postures of the body designed to increase muscle strength, flexibility, and relaxation. It is often coupled with meditation and deep breathing techniques. Classes can be found with certified instructors in most communities.

Massage

Massage is the application of pressure, rubbing and kneading of muscles and other soft body tissues to produce a therapeutic effect, which includes reduction in muscle tension. Massage helps to alleviate muscle soreness and pain, and will produce an overall state of relaxation. Other benefits may include the release of body toxins, and improvement in circulation, blood pressure, and mood. A licensed massage therapist can be easily accessed in most communities.

Medication

The use of prescribed medication from a licensed physician is not the same as drinking or using street drugs, and you shouldn't feel embarrassed if you choose this option. Medication may be what you need to take the edge off of your symptoms and become more amenable to verbal therapy with helpful behavioral activities.

Anxiolytic medication is another name for anti-anxiety agents. It may be a prescribed benzodiazepine, such as the well-known brand names of *Valium, Xanax, Klonopin, Librium,* or *Ativan.* These medications work fairly quickly and are frequently prescribed for short-term use because of concern about physiological dependence and potential for abuse. Other medications, such as beta-receptor blockers and antidepressants have also successfully found their way into the treatment of anxiety.

Your doctor has a lot of choices when working with you to find the right medication regimen to manage your symptoms. Many general practitioners feel more comfortable referring you to a specialist, such as a psychiatrist, who has expertise in *psychopharmacology*. Being under proper medical supervision is important for your health. Asking questions and being a self-advocate is always wise. So, talk to your doctor and understand your treatment plan. Let him or her know that you are working with a therapist and provide the necessary written permission to allow an exchange of information. It is better to have a team approach and keep in mind that you are also part of this team.

17

Depression

Whether it is called *melancholia* or the deep blues, depression can come on like a storm with dark clouds. It does not discriminate; anyone can suffer from it. Over 300 million people worldwide experience some form of depression. For some, it comes and goes in episodes and for others it seems to be an enduring state. The level of severity and symptoms may vary from person to person. However, when your mood stays down and you are unable to function in everyday life, depression has hit you hard and it's time to get professional help.

What are the symptoms of *depression*? That depends on the type of depression you have. *Major depression*, as its clinical name implies, refers to a profound sense of despair with feelings of intense sadness, emptiness and a strong desire to frequently break out in tears. It may also be characterized by a loss of interest and pleasure in usual activities. So, you may not feel like going out with friends or enjoying a social event that once gave you happiness. In fact, you may find yourself isolating from others or shutting off from the rest of the world. Your whole being seems to be affected by this condition. You may be unable to get to sleep, or constantly wake up in the middle of the night and in the early morning hours. You may feel too tired and unmotivated to get yourself out of bed. You may have no appetite and lose a significant amount of weight. Some people find themselves eating too much and gaining weight rapidly. Your energy may be depleted and you feel fatigued most, if not all, of the time. You may also be unusually irritable and get easily agitated by the slightest thing. Your body may be either slowed down or aimlessly moving about. Your concentration may be affected where you are unable to think through problems or you find yourself becoming anxious and forgetful. You may have an unwarranted sense of guilt, or a serious drop in self-esteem with feelings of worthlessness. Some people experience unexplainable physical ailments with pain. When mood swings are present and depression is accompanied or replaced by episodes of *mania* (euphoria and/or agitation), this is called *bipolar disorder* (formerly known as *manic depression*).

Of all the symptoms that come with major depression, recurrent thoughts of death or suicide, called *suicidal ideation*, can become a frightening addition to the clinical picture. When feeling helpless and hopeless, you may think this is your only option. Having a specific plan and access to weapons or other potentially lethal items (like a gun, rope, or pills) makes the situation high-risk and cause for immediate attention. Avoid alcohol or any mood altering street drugs. Don't be afraid to talk with your therapist about any suicidal thoughts or intentions.

If you have these feelings of suicidal ideation, and they are strong, you are in danger. Under these conditions, it would be necessary to get an emergency mental health evaluation. Because of its seriousness, there is the possibility of a temporary hospital admission. Entering the hospital would be for your safety and benefit. If unable to reach your therapist, it is best to find your way to the nearest hospital emergency room. Calling a supportive family member or friend to accompany you is a good idea. Again, don't be afraid or embarrassed to tell the emergency staff about your problem and why you are there. They are experienced medical professionals and you are not the first person they've encountered feeling this way. Trust me, no matter what else you may think, your family and friends would rather you spend a brief time in the hospital during this very dark period. It certainly trumps the shocking and preventable alternative with its unspeakable permanence.

Later, as you feel better, and you will feel better, you will come to regret ever having considered suicide. You will begin to value the presence and support of your family and friends. Over time, you will also value what the present and future has to offer.

Remember, being extremely negative in your thoughts is a hallmark trait of depression and it is extremely harmful. If a crisis situation were to happen to you, recognize that it is all part of a very serious condition called major depression. Choose life! Take positive action and keep moving forward. Work on looking at and appreciating the positives in your life as you move forward. It may take some doing, but it is not impossible to push out the pessimism and embrace the optimism. What would you advise a friend?

One person writing into a popular magazine spoke honestly about her experience of depression and suicidal urges. She noted how even mental health professionals who frequently deal with this issue don't always have a true understanding of it. She also offered words of hope and optimism. Please note the following insightful comments written by a depression survivor:

As someone who attempted suicide herself, I think the constant focus put on pain by psychologists and those in the medical community often misses the mark. Pain for me and for many others is the step before. Complete inability to feel anything or to connect with anyone was the point where sui-

cide became more of a reality to me. I was a ghost in my body, not really there anyway, and felt as if I was a burden on my family and would never get better. Luckily, I did not have access to a gun, and my attempts were not successful. Doing well for years. There are ways out of that level of depression—it is just unique for each person.

—Julie K. Hersh (2013)

As I've already stated, depression may come and go in discrete episodes or it may stay with you as more diffuse and less intense. Many of my clients revealed suffering from it for as long as they could remember. Somehow, these clients were able to get by, but with a feeling that something was lacking or missing. For much of the time they experienced a feeling of sadness and low self-esteem. They also complained of having difficulties with energy, concentration, sleep, appetite, and negative thinking. In the psychiatric nomenclature, this is a condition called *dysthymia*. Previously, it was referred to as a *depressive neurosis*.

Dysthymia is like having a long-term low-grade fever that doesn't seem to go away. There may be brief periods of normal mood, but overall that lingering sense of sadness remains and goes on for years. Although this is a troubling condition, it's milder than major depression. I've known many people struggling with it, yet still relatively successful in their careers and family lives. If you recognize this type of depression in yourself, it's worth looking for professional help. Psychotherapy can be very useful.

The operative word when talking about depression in psychodynamic terms is *loss*. It can result from the death of a loved one, divorce, broken relationship, transfer or termination of employment, or a significant change in health. It can come from parental neglect or abuse in childhood (loss of nurturance and love), school failure or social rejection. It can come from the loss of what once was—a lost reality, or once wished—lost hopes and dreams. Grief and bereavement are common terms when we talk about loss; they describe a natural reaction and factor into the healing process. Needless to say, loss is inevitable and a part of living.

I learned many years ago, while attending social work school, that mental health problems are closely related to problems in living. The model of *person-in-situation* was presented at that time to help us understand that we are all individuals constantly interacting with our environment. In addition to our own biology, we are faced with family, social, financial, legal, cultural, and other challenges. You can't live your life and expect all aspects to always go well! As I've said before, adversity or problems in living will eventually come to all of us, whether it is early in life or later. Sooner or later, we will all need to cope with unexpected and unwelcome stress.

When external factors lead to a severe lowering of mood and functioning, depression is said to be the result of *exogenous* factors. It is a good idea to talk with your therapist about your stressors and discuss strategies of coping. You may need to do some grief work before moving on to your next challenge. It will prepare you to tackle whatever else may come your way.

However, depression also has *endogenous* or internal factors. Here, brain chemistry gets upset and severely imbalanced. Chemicals in the brain, such as, *serotonin, norepinephrine,* and *dopamine* have all been noted to have a significant role with mood regulation. Lower levels of these chemicals have been found in the brain of the depressed person. Other endogenous factors contributing to depression include variations in the release of hormones, and the body's chemical response from intake of drugs, alcohol, or other toxins.

Various medical conditions are also known to cause depression, such as *hypoglycemia, hypothyroidism, vitamin B12* deficiency, *stroke, multiple sclerosis, Alzheimer's dementia*, and *Parkinson's disease*, to name a few. Depression has also been associated with cardiac conditions and events.

While this is not an all-inclusive list of brain chemicals and medical illnesses, it certainly gives you an idea of how the body can break down and, in turn, get you down. It supports the argument for a good physical exam when one notices a significant change in mood and behavior. It is certainly a time of alert, a time to see your doctor. A physical exam is always recommended before seeing a therapist. Your doctor may find a medical condition and treat it with diet or medications. That might be all you need. However, if depression persists and is the primary diagnosis, you may be a candidate for antidepressant medication.

Antidepressants are a group of medications specifically designed to target depression and reduce or eliminate the symptoms. Your doctor may prescribe one or more of these to help you get better. If medication is recommended, follow your doctor's advice and give it a try. Keep in mind that these medications may take a few weeks to kick in for positive results. Don't give up on them too quickly.

Also keep in mind that the best practice for treatment of depression is not medication alone. When medication is indicated, it is best to use it in combination with talk therapy. This is a well-known fact! It is important for you to work with a therapist and talk about what's bothering you. This is a time to figure out how to begin "thinking and doing" things differently. It is a time to take a new path. Again, give your talk therapy some time to work. Don't get impatient and give up too soon!

What will you be dealing with in talk therapy for depression? *Cognitive behavioral therapy*, specifically the approach of REBT pioneered by Albert Ellis, is an effective approach for depression (see chapter 8). Additionally, a psychiatrist by the name of Aaron T. Beck did groundbreaking work in the field, particularly when it comes to the study and treatment of depression. Beck, also known as the father of *cognitive therapy*, introduced the *cognitive triad*. He observed that a depressed person harbored very negative and dysfunctional views about *the self, the world*, and *the future*. Thoughts would be filled with ideas about being worthless, the world as unfair, and the future as hopeless. Since cognitive therapy is based on the premise that depression is caused by distorted thinking, the work of therapy would therefore be to change these depressive-causing beliefs.

Consistent with REBT and the cognitive approach to working with depression is Paul Hauck's very helpful and readable book for those who suffer with this emotional disturbance, titled *Overcoming Depression* (1973). Hauck was enamored by the creative genius of Ellis and dedicated the book to him. He suggested that a person suffering with depression may have one or more of three contributing causes: self-blame, self-pity, and other-pity. As expected, a key to reducing or eliminating the disturbance is to identify which of these pertain to the depression being experienced, and then to vigorously work on defeating those cognitions and related behaviors.

Remember, depression is a treatable condition. Your full cooperation in partnership with your therapist and professional team is needed to improve the prognosis and achieve success. When you feel lousy, you may not want to do anything to help yourself or you may think that "it's just no use." Your therapist may assign homework to help overcome your low motivation.

Starting a physical exercise program may be recommended to get your body moving. Pushing yourself to attend various social and recreational activities that you once considered pleasurable may be part of the plan to help you get better. Purposefully engaging in these types of actions, even when you feel you don't want to, is called *behavioral activation*. At first you may have doubts that any of these activities can help you feel better, but once you try them, you learn that they actually do.

Writing logs and journals may also help you to look at your current point of view and consider how it jibes with reality. It will be a gradual process of evolving manageable steps. The whole point is to undo the negative distortions of your depressed frame of mind and to begin accepting a much healthier and improved reality. This will change your perceptions from darkness to light. Take it from me and countless others, you will be thankful that you actively participated in your treatment, and so will your family and friends.

18
Anger

What triggers your *anger*? Many clients have come to me with surprisingly little insight about this emotion. They had difficulty controlling their anger because they really didn't know the first thing about it and took no ownership. Most of them spoke about how others or external events just "make me angry," and "they deserved what they got." When these clients reached my office, they came involuntarily and saw counseling only as a way to fulfill a legal mandate. Some were referred by a criminal court judge after participating in a physical fight or brawl in the community. Others were sent from a family court while settling a separation or divorce decree after multiple episodes of screaming, fighting, hitting, destroying property, and "burning rubber" by speeding off in a car.

When anger gets explosive, violent, destructive and uncontrollable it will lead to serious self-defeating consequences including loss of relationships, jobs, legal problems, and a host of other difficulties. Suppressed anger may contribute or lead to various stress related health conditions, such as *migraine headaches*, *backaches*, *stomach ulcers*, and *high blood pressure*.

When anger gets in the way of normal living, it's time to do something about it. If outbursts are too frequent or too intense, anger is controlling you rather than the other way around. If aggression is part of your expressed anger, now is the time to take a look at yourself, admit that your reactions are *maladaptive* and consider the need to change. You may be hurting yourself and others without really admitting to it. Don't let this happen! It's easy to downplay your behavior and make all kinds of excuses. I see this all the time in my practice.

Controlling your anger means that you don't have to automatically "go off" on someone when things don't go your way. Aggression, which is behavior intended to damage something or harm someone, does not have to be a part of expressing your irritation. "Blacking out" and losing yourself in the moment is no excuse. It will not hold up in court, and it will not prevent you from ultimately facing the consequences. Isn't it time to start taking responsibility for your behavior? There are other ways to get what you want without causing so much trouble. You can also learn how to live when it is not possible to get what you want.

Before discussing types of anger and ways of coping, it is important to encourage you to take good care of yourself. Know your personal needs and how to satisfy them. When you are too hungry, tired, or overwhelmed by excessive stress, the natural response is to feel uptight and less tolerant. Pay attention to your mind and body by getting the right amount of nutrition, sleep, rest, and relaxation.

The dynamics of anger require much more time and space than I'm affording here, but it's worth a brief discussion. Anger can be explained as deriving from an unmet *demand* where the individual thinks that something *must* or *must not* happen.

When Julius came in to see me it was because his wife insisted that he do something other than "scream and yell at the kids." She wanted him to stop "throwing things" and "throwing his temper around." Every day, he would come home from work to find a mess in the kitchen after the kids helped themselves to an afternoon snack.

"Why can't they clean up after themselves?" he would ask with irritation. Julius complained loudly and *demanded* that these kids must change despite his wife's acceptance of their behavior. The more he ranted and raved, the less it worked to get him what he wanted. He was especially upset by his wife's betrayal of his wishes and her alliance with the kids. He felt disrespected by the whole family. As parents, they did not have a unified front and so the negative behavioral pattern continued. Naturally, the marriage began to disintegrate and anger loomed everywhere.

When an attack is perceived on one's ego, the expected human reaction is anger. This is what happened with Julius when he felt the loss of status as a father and husband. Unfortunately, his reactive anger backfired. When someone is disrespected, ignored, treated punitively, insulted, threatened, or violated, anger emerges.

Another form of anger one readily sees is when Joe and Mary arrive for a typical social visit. Somehow the topic always turns to politics and they feel compelled to express their very strong opinions. If they hear ideas contrary to their own, both become indignant and darn right hostile. They see all others as narrow-minded, inflexible, and stupid. Yet, they are the ones who are rigid and unwilling to accept other points of view. They disregard the freedom of speech and choice of others. Disagree with what they have to say and you will pay a price. Joe and Mary always claim to take the moral high ground and are determined to prove their position with *self-righteous anger*. What they haven't yet noticed is their dwindling social network. Fewer and fewer friends are inviting them to social events.

After recognizing that your anger is maladaptive, what more

can you do? Admitting that you have a problem is an important first step. The next step is developing greater awareness and objectivity around the problem. Finally, you need to learn how to apply coping skills for *anger management*, including *self-monitoring* as a key factor for success.

When you can identify what *triggers* your excessive anger, you can start using your coping skills. Most people try to avoid these triggers, if at all possible. This is a simple solution that is very useful and recommended as an initial coping strategy. A more elegant approach would be to recognize what lies behind your response to these triggers, and then learn how to effectively deal with it. It is best to go over the specifics of a situation and work it through with your therapist. Together, you will find how your distorted thinking leads to your anger. It is your thinking that will undoubtedly turn out to be the real culprit. The idea is to parse through the unhealthy thoughts leading to your anger and work on accepting a new perspective, one that is healthier and self-enhancing. This process of cognitive restructuring will help you to consider an alternative point of view. To stubbornly refuse a fresher view on things will only keep you stuck!

Although you will be working with your therapist, you will still need to handle yourself when it is not practical to avoid triggering situations. Under such circumstances, it is essential to catch your anger before it escalates out of control. What tells you that you are getting upset? Do you get cues from your body, such as heavy breathing, tightened muscles, clenched teeth or fists? Do you tense up, "see red," and have destructive thoughts? Do you feel hurt, irritated, and vulnerable? Are you unable to remain calm and "stay put" because you think that you must make a move or take some action? Just as you monitor the triggers that provoke your anger, monitoring how you react will help you to de-escalate it. If you catch it early, you can prevent yourself from exploding. Once you've reached a state of rage, it's too late. By that time, the damage is done and the consequences are on their way.

Do you have an *anger plan*? The beginning of your plan for self-control is to recognize when you are heating up and about to boil over. Besides paying attention to your triggering events, thoughts, and bodily cues, I would suggest taking your *anger temperature*. Using a subjective scale from 0 to 10 and rating yourself is an excellent way of deciding how angry you are feeling at any given time. You can then decide what you need to do, using various possibilities available for coping.

In the following sections you'll find some strategies to address your anger. Some might work better than others, but keep an open mind and consider how useful they may be for you.

Timeout

Timeout is a way of removing yourself from the triggering situation for a long enough time to cool off and calm down. You may want to take a walk or a run by yourself. It is helpful to use self-talk reminding yourself to be calm, dignified and not act out in a destructive manner. During a timeout you can think about and imagine a more constructive approach to the conflict at hand.

Thought Stopping

When your anger becomes excessive, you are likely to have aggressive thoughts and images. This is a good time to take a deep breath and visualize a "stop sign" in your mind's eye. Called *thought stopping*, doing so will interrupt the flow of these aggressive cognitions. Again, self-talk, self-instruction, and coping statements are all part of this action. After imagining the stop sign, firmly tell yourself to "stop." You will also want to tell yourself, "These angry thoughts and images only make matters worse!" and "I'm not going to follow that dangerous path!"

Try to remember a time when you were challenged but successfully controlled yourself. It is proof that you can do it! Start thinking that you deserve better. You are above and beyond that kind of undignified behavior that leads into serious trouble. You can do better and will do better!

Combining thought stopping with imagery can be especially effective. Try to think of an alternative experience, one that is more soothing and calming for you. Think of a warm, friendly, and safe place, a pleasant memory from your past. It can be a sandy beach with mild ocean waves and a warm gentle breeze. It can be the comfort and safety of your home, in your room holding a blanket, soft pillow, or favorite stuffed animal toy from childhood. It can be enjoying your pet, reading a book, or watching a favorite movie. Whatever works for you is the best way of choosing what to think of and re-experience. The idea is to stop the aggressive thoughts and calm yourself down.

Assertive Communication

When you make threats or allow explosive rage to take over, you act in a way that tramples on the rights of others. This aggressive behavior will come with negative consequences. On the other side, when you are too passive, then you don't give yourself enough credit or fail to project a message that your thoughts and feelings count. Others will take advantage of the situation and you may feel exploited. However, when you appropriately stand up for yourself without anger and aggression, this is called being assertive. Learning how to engage in *assertive communication* is sometimes called *assertiveness training* when done with a therapist.

You will find this approach to be practical and very effective. It is not done by being nasty, confrontational, raising the volume of your voice, or intruding in the personal space of others. Rather, it is more correctly practiced with poise by keeping eye contact, holding a straight posture, and calmly stating your case to the other person in a rational manner. It is important to be composed and confident. You want to be persistent and hold tight to your position unless compromise is more appropriate. The idea is to not get defeated or lose your position. It is helpful to think about and rehearse what to say prior to the contact. You want to always be clear, concise, and eloquent but mindful of the feelings and rights of others during your conversation. Respect is an essential part of assertive behavior and will guide the tone of your approach.

Let Go of the Demand

As difficult as this is to believe, the harsh truth is that your demanding nature is the strongest factor of why you get yourself so worked up and angry. You may want to control everyone and everything to get your way. Such an absolute strategy just won't work, and that means sometimes you'll need to *let go of the demand*.

So, just why do others have to do what you want? You will find that *free will* tends to dictate the behavior of others, and this may not always fit with your own expectations or perceived needs. So, again, why *must* you get what you want? Granted it would be nice if you did and life would certainly be easier if the world really worked that way. You would never ever feel frustrated! But the fact is that the world, and everyone in it, works and carries on independently of you. Rest assured, the world will still be there once you and I are long gone. If it so happens to meet your needs or you can tactfully find a way to get what you want from it, good for you. Many times, however, it won't work that way.

An old saying and one that I heard from my own mother quite often is, "You'll just have to lump it!" Perhaps more modern slang that you've occasionally heard goes like this: "Just suck it up!" Sometimes life isn't fair. And often things are just not in our control, no matter how much we try to manipulate or how strong we insist that they have to go our way. Our world is not always predictable and perfect. That's what makes life so interesting, a journey more enjoyed by those who are flexible— those who have learned to *let go* of the things they are unable to change. To let go of the demand that things must go your way, you achieve the freedom to feel more at peace and behave in a much calmer more deliberate manner. It is a way to take back your power!

Problem Solving

Having unresolved problems is stressful. It often results in lower frustration tolerance and an increase in anger. Do you notice how impatient you get when you have problems hanging over your head and you are feeling stressed? The beauty of *problem solving* is that it offers a relatively simple five-step process that will help you to really look at a situation objectively and consider ways of approaching it. The process forces you to think more clearly and creatively to reach your goal. It is better to use paper and pencil to write it all down, as this enables a better analysis. Here are the steps in a nutshell:

1. *Identify the problem.* What is really bothering you about the situation? How does it affect you practically and emotionally? What are the specifics? Who else is involved? How are they affected?
2. *Brainstorm possible solutions.* Think of ways to solve the problem and create a list of choices. What can you do to fix the problem? What else might work?
3. *Evaluate the solutions.* Take a look at each choice on your list. Consider both the pros and cons. Keep in mind that not all problems have perfect answers.
4. *Pick one and try it out.* Of course, you should select the one solution that is expected to give the best possible results. This is the one with more pros, and where the argu-

ments in favor of it are the most convincing.

5. *Evaluate the results.* After trying it out, did the solution work? If it did then you have successfully used the problem solving process to your advantage. Congratulations! If the solution you picked didn't do the job (step 3), it's time to rethink, and maybe try another one (step 4). Is the problem clear and well formulated enough? Do you need to redefine the problem (step 1)? Is there a more constructive solution that you have not yet considered (step 2)? Are you expecting too much too soon from the solution? Does it need more time and repetition? Do you need to consult with someone who can take a fresh look at the situation?

When using this problem solving process for conflict resolution with another person, it involves meeting with that person to address the problem by discussing it thoroughly, learning how it affects both of you, and working collaboratively to resolve the issue. Beware that this may not always be received well by the other person and you may have to tread lightly with some level of diplomacy. You may need to negotiate a less than perfect solution where both parties compromise. You may also find that the other person is just too stubborn and will not want this type of discussion with you. This is why it is always wise to "pick your battles" and know which ones are just not important enough for you to pursue. A smart man once said, "If you expect perfection from all your friends, you will have no friends."

When Lois hears a statement from her mother that she doesn't like, she says, "Mom, stop!" Sometimes she screams back, accusing her mother of not "hearing" or "listening." Raising her voice and being confrontational has been damaging to the mother–daughter relationship over the years. More recently, Lois has cut phone calls short by abruptly hanging up. She never learned to calmly express herself around her mother, or to accept the fact that sometimes they will need to resolve their differences by agreeing to disagree.

Mother has become very careful around her daughter and says, "It's like walking on thin ice." Mother feels tense with mixed feelings about their encounters. Although she loves her daughter, she dreads the negative contacts. This is not the way to develop a growing loving relationship. Is it time for the two of them to sit down with a therapist and iron out their problems? Can Lois discuss her built-up resentments and move on from there? Would learning conflict resolution skills be of any help?

Passive-Aggressive Behavior

I want to say a few words about *passive-aggressive behavior*. This is essentially an expression of aggressive hostility "through the back door." The person showing this behavior is usually dealing with some type of authority, such as a parent, boss, or teacher. It also turns up in relationships with spouses and even friends. Passive-aggressive behavior can take many forms, including *passive resistance, intentional inefficiency, obstructionism,* or *procrastination.* The person uses this behavior in place of an open expression of anger, being fearful of its immediate consequences. He is unable to be assertive, and often dependent on the relationship.

Examples of this include an employee repeatedly coming late for supervision meetings, a student frequently losing his homework, or a gardener intentionally leaving a pile of debris at the end of the job. You can probably think of many more examples and be my guest to do so! If you are displaying this behavior on a regular basis, think about what it is doing to you and your relationships. Don't be stubborn about it! Aren't there other ways to feel a sense of power and dignity without using this subversive approach? Do you need to discuss this with your therapist?

Finally, long term *seething anger* is a condition that begs for an act of vengeance or revenge. People living with this consider their real or fantasized actions as a form of justice. This claim is actually moral confusion. They believe that doing harm to another will somehow wipe the slate clean and fulfill the dictum of "an eye for an eye." They become the judge and jury all rolled into one. Before acting on pure emotion, stop and ask yourself some important questions: What am I doing? Is it worth it? Can I change the past? Do two wrongs make a right? Can I let go and move on? Can I forgive? Forgiving will likely take some time and can be a very difficult thing to do. It takes deep introspection and perhaps a reliance on spiritual strength.

Now, try to constructively use this newly acquired knowledge to gain insight and get free of your anger. It's a curse you can do without. Work on feeling more joyful! That's a much better way to live your life.

19

Psychosis and Psychotic Mood Disorders

I have seen hundreds of people suffering with severe mental illness during my 30-plus years of working within the public mental health system. This included *schizophrenic, schizoaffective*, and *bipolar disorders*. What they all have in common is a brain disorder with severe breakdown in psychosocial functioning. This means that it is extremely difficult for them to do the everyday tasks of living, including self-care, work at a regular job and socialization, which most of us take for granted.

Episodes of these disorders appear in late adolescence and early adult life, just when one is developing an identity and preparing for a future with relationships and career. When the illness hits, it is unusually confusing and devastating to the individual and his or her family. Periods of illness may come and go, and they may initially appear insidious and progressive. When the disorder becomes chronic, long-term treatment is required.

Those afflicted may lose insight about their situation and become uncooperative, denying any problems, and unwilling to seek out help or stay in treatment. The one certainty is a very noticeable and extreme change in behavior. They may be seen doing things out of the ordinary, such as talking to themselves, looking at others with undue suspicion, or isolating and distancing themselves by spending more time alone, closing off from the world, and appearing more apathetic than ever before.

What are the symptoms that develop and interfere with a normal life? Let's start with *impaired reality testing*. People who suffer with these illnesses get very confused about what is real. Perceptions of reality get distorted, as the brain has difficulty filtering and interpreting experiences through the senses. They have problems with thinking, concentrating, and communicating. Thoughts become disorganized, loose, and scattered. Speech contains peculiar content or appears unusually rapid and difficult to understand. *Delusions* may develop, which are false ideas about reality. These delusions are rigidly held onto by the individual and usually do not respond to logic or reasoning.

There are various types of delusions, depending on condition and mood state. *Paranoid delusions* are commonly observed where one feels targeted for persecution from others. The person may feel like a victim of a conspiracy, malevolent plot, or some other evil force. Delusions can be bizarre, such as the belief of being controlled by aliens through radio waves, thoughts telepathically inserted into the brain, or thoughts being broadcast over media for public scrutiny. There may be a strong religious preoccupation with the belief in a connection to a particular deity or being chosen to receive godly messages.

When experiencing *grandiose delusions*, the person will have thoughts of being particularly unique or special, outside of what is considered normal self-confidence. I once treated a person with bipolar disorder who walked through town believing that he was a real estate magnate. He falsely told people that he owned several buildings and rental properties. Because of his *mania*, he quickly got into trouble and found himself in town court facing legal charges of public mischief. During his court hearing, he told the judge that he was not in need of a court-appointed attorney because he too was a lawyer, able to defend himself. Of course, this idea was conjured up during his state of *manic euphoria.*

Although this client was mostly pleasant, mania may sometimes come with a great deal of agitation and disturbed behavior. It is always with excessive energy, reduced need for sleep, rapid speech, and unrestrained involvement in pleasurable activities, which frequently results in self-defeating or negative consequences. People suffering with manic episodes have been known to go on huge spending sprees, gambling escapades, or run off on highly expensive and poorly planned trips. They may drive a car dangerously fast, have unprotected sex with multiple partners, get into fights, abuse substances, or make incredibly poor business decisions. There is no doubt about it, that unstable mood clearly leads to unstable behavior with very poor judgment.

People suffering with major mental illness may also struggle with *depressive delusions.* The case of Olivia offers a good illustration of this. She came to our clinic for follow-up care shortly after being discharged from the local hospital. The admission note indicated that she had stopped eating and lost a considerable amount of weight. A comprehensive physical exam revealed no medical abnormalities. But Olivia believed that her stomach was withering away from a ravaging disease and the world was coming to a sudden end. She also expressed ideas of having committed unforgivable sins for which she was unable to repent. Olivia presented to hospital staff with both *somatic delusions,* beliefs that her body was not functioning properly despite evidence to the contrary, and *nihilistic delusions,* beliefs that parts of her body were dying. Fortunately, she responded to a medication regimen and supportive therapy. After a period of stabilization, she was referred for further rehabilitation services.

Hallucinations may also be part of the clinical profile when psychosis is present. This is when a person hears, sees, smells, tastes, or feels something that is not experienced by others. It is clearly part of the illness and is very real for the person having the hallucinations. Auditory hallucinations appear to be the most common. For example, the person suffering the illness may hear an ongoing dialogue of voices, specific commands, or shouting insults. Can you imagine having to participate in a work environment, family activity or social event while hearing these distracting voices? They may come at varying intervals with changes in volume and emotional intensity. Hallucinations seriously interfere with concentration, already a problem that comes with the illness. It makes coping with normal life almost impossible.

In the 1980's, I ran several *psychoeducation* groups for parents and family members of clients suffering with mental illness. I received expert help by a very competent psychiatric nurse at that time. Together, we provided valuable information and ways of navigating within the confusing system of care. We offered a lot of emotional support to these group members—most of all, we listened to them. One mother gave a personal account of her initial encounter with mental illness in the family. It was a striking and heartbreaking story:

My son was 19 when we got the call from his college. He was getting ready for his sophomore year. When we got there he was acting very strange. He was "wide-eyed" and kept looking away from us, as if he was distracted by voices in his head. His comments didn't seem to be making much sense. I knew he was scared but he showed very little emotion. He wasn't taking care of himself very well; he was neglecting his personal hygiene.

*Fortunately, he was willing to come with us to the hospi-
tal emergency room. He was admitted to the psychiatric floor
and this is how our journey with mental illness began. They
kept him there a couple of weeks. We were told by the doctor
and social worker that he has schizophrenia and would need
to be in treatment for the rest of his life. He was prescribed
medications that have a lot of side effects. Sometimes it's a
struggle to get him to take them. He seems slowed down and
gained a lot of weight.*

*He now sees his doctor and social worker at the clinic on
a regular basis. We met with them too. They seem like good
people who want to help him but this illness has its ups and
downs. Some days are better than others. They are trying to
get him into a program to keep busy during the day rather than staying home and spending most of the time lying
around. I hope this happens soon.*

*This illness has changed everything. My son was supposed
to finish college, have a career, meet a nice girl, get married
and live a normal happy life. Our hopes and dreams for him
went right out the window. We don't know what the future
will bring but we do know that life in this family is not as it
was intended to be. It has changed forever and I'm not sure
we will ever recover. He didn't deserve this and neither did
we.*

—J.R.V.

While genetic predisposition and stress appear to be contributing factors, abnormal levels of neurotransmitter chemicals in the brain are thought to be the biological cause of
psychosis. These chemicals include *dopamine, glutamate,* and
serotonin. The study of what causes psychosis is obviously complicated and it is hopeful that one day we'll know for sure the
mechanisms driving these mental illnesses.

Where do you go for help with a problem like this? Of course, when anyone gets sick in the family it is always a good idea to start with the family doctor. After a complete physical examination, he or she will determine whether to provide a referral to a psychiatrist. If the situation is at a crisis level, get to a hospital emergency room. It's better to go to a hospital that has a psychiatric department. If the situation cannot be handled through private psychiatric care, there may be a need to connect with the public mental health system. Usually this is a complex system providing a wide array of supportive services from case management to housing. The public mental health clinic is staffed with practitioners to offer medication, counseling, and referrals.

Don't forget to ask about an education and support group for family members. If there is no group available at the clinic, there may be one at another site sponsored by the local division of the National Alliance on Mental Illness (NAMI).

20

Insight Is
Not Enough

Most people who enter therapy just want to know *why* they feel or act the way they do. They are looking for a better understanding of themselves, and believe that somehow this will translate into change. While this may work for some, others are left bewildered by their lack of progress, despite having a clearer perspective on how their past has shaped their present. Rather than ask the age-old question of "Why?" it is better to ask a couple of other questions: "What do I want to change?" and "How can I make this change come about?"

It's been over four decades since psychiatrist Maxie C. Maultsby, Jr., taught us how to take responsibility for improving our state of being. He pointed out that we could make ourselves feel a whole lot better and do a whole lot better by looking at the nonsense in our heads and changing it into *rational thinking*. He was talking to those who felt helpless about their conditions and told them that they didn't have to sit back and suffer. They could clearly do something about it by being proactive. By giving up old habits and faulty thinking, he suggested that one could say "goodbye" to emotional disturbance and negative behaviors.

Maultsby was a proponent of *rational self analysis* (RSA), a procedure recognizing five characteristics of rational thoughts. Taken as questions, these characteristics can be used to dispute one's original self-defeating beliefs. These are the five questions:

1. Does it hold true?
2. Does it lead me to protect my life and health?
3. Does it get me what I want?
4. Does it keep me out of trouble?
5. Does it keep me feeling the way I want to feel?

After isolating core thoughts and scrutinizing them based on these questions, one is better able to decide whether to keep or toss them in favor of a healthier more rational self.

Peggy came to me suffering from mood swings and difficulty regulating her emotions. She often felt either depressed or angry, and this was usually about some type of relationship issue. She was always threatened by the possibility of abandonment from a friend. She was never really sure of herself and lacked a solid feeling of identity. She would manipulate situations to end up as an underdog and then dramatically whine about her victimization.

Peggy couldn't undo these habitual patterns of emotion and behavior by merely knowing about their existence or by understanding how they originated. Peggy had a hard life as the only child of a depressed woman. Her mother was unable to give enough nurturing for Peggy to feel truly loved. As a little girl, Peggy would return home from school in the late afternoon to find her mother still in bed, depressed and withdrawn from the world. Peggy found herself very much alone and having strong feelings that "I don't count." She would joke in sessions, "My membership card in the human race was never stamped and validated." These thoughts were etched into her mind and clearly had an impact on how she related to herself, others, and the world around her. Having insight about where her feelings came from in the past might have given her a better understanding of why she felt the way she did, but it had little bearing on helping her feel better in the future.

Another example where insight was just not enough was the case of Joshua. He had been driving a car and stopped at a traffic light, waiting for it to turn green. Suddenly, his car was hit from behind and his head was pushed back with whiplash. He suffered injury to his neck and back but was lucky that it wasn't serious and permanent. After a few weeks, he was able to physically recover and he was medically cleared to return to work.

However, the accident was not going away and it stayed as a haunting experience in his mind. He had flashbacks about it and got quite anxious. He would wonder: "What if I had been crippled for life?" He began withdrawing, fearful about leaving his apartment and nervous about driving his car. He began avoiding the corner where the accident happened and took a different route to get to his therapy sessions. He recognized that these changes were not good and that he was developing a serious problem. It all overwhelmed him. He was worried about becoming an "emotional invalid" and didn't want this to happen. He was afraid that he would be unable to return to work or move forward with his life.

Both Peggy and Joshua clearly had irrational thoughts but they were bright enough to identify and work on them. As Maultsby, Ellis, Beck, Meichenbaum, and so many other cognitive-behavioral therapists tell us, challenging an idea in your head is only the beginning to an end. You must act on your new rational idea in order to change it into a belief! Once you own this new belief, you have achieved attitudinal change and new behavior will naturally go with it. Peggy had to work very hard at self-affirmations, and developing more genuine trust in her relationships. Joshua was anxious but had to tolerate increased arousal as he faced his fears. He realized that he needed to drive his car and even take the route where his troubles all began. He learned a very valuable lesson in therapy. Change is based on rethinking and then doing, doing, doing!

Why are all these therapeutic steps necessary in order to achieve change? It is because of how the human brain is built and works. The brain is our executive organ and engaging in cognitive-restructuring exercises helps make it work to our advantage.

Scientists are learning more about the brain every day. Modern technology, using imaging such as *magnetic resonance imaging* (MRI) and *computed tomography* (CT) scans, shows that activity in the brain changes through our life experiences. Memories and reactions get formed over a lifetime and these are recorded in the brain by a process called *neuroplasticity*. This was first noted in the field of *rehabilitation*, where the brain made adjustments for victims of stroke, accidents, and *traumatic brain injuries* (TBI's).

One might consider neuroplasticity as the physiologic equivalent of resilience. People do get better with treatment over time, though their functioning may not always reach its previous level. When faced with serious life stressors such as loss, trauma, or a major disturbing event, physical changes occur in the brain. We are all "hot-wired" by nature to possess a complex system with billions of interacting neurons fired up by electrical and chemical energy. New message paths are formed, which translate into our human reactions. In short, we automatically adapt to these stressful experiences by creating new neurological paths. This happens automatically, without our even being aware of it.

What happens when your reaction to life stressors becomes excessive fear, avoidance, depression, or anger? The new brain paths may be considered troublesome and maladaptive, especially if they don't change with the passing of time. It becomes an uncomfortable though familiar pattern of interacting with the environment. However, with knowledge and conscious effort, it is possible to navigate and construct new brain paths that are less troublesome and more adaptive. This requires determination and effort that goes beyond simple awareness or insight. It requires an active approach of changing cognitions (thoughts and beliefs) and behaviors. These new brain paths then take hold, with new ways of viewing the world, and newly learned behaviors to cope with the world.

Pushing yourself to change behaviors may feel awkward or uncomfortable at first. However, it is very important that your newer and healthier behaviors (the things you do) are consistent with your newer and healthier cognitions (the thoughts you have). These changes in behavior will serve to reinforce your new belief system. They work hand in hand. Once you are thinking and believing differently, it will show up as a more appropriate attitude and world view. It will be a metamorphosis well worth the effort.

Your therapist has methods, techniques, and strategies to help you develop these new brain paths. Be committed to your therapy and work hard. Do homework assignments and understand why they are important. As you know from reading thus far, you'll be asked to do a lot of self-monitoring, write self-help forms, practice relaxation exercises, and much more. Whatever it is, review any difficulties you encounter and revise the assignments accordingly to do better each and every time. Your ultimate goal is to gain a greater mastery of these tasks because they are the building blocks to a newer improved self.

You may have to do things over and over again. And you may experience some frustration. Remember, repetition is part of the learning process and re-education is what we are after for the success of your therapy. So, work hard, stick with it, have some faith, try to have some fun, and good luck on your journey!

Part V

—

*Other Things
to Consider*

21

Spiritual and Religious Beliefs

When considering *spirituality* and *religion*, I first thought that I was the wrong person to write this chapter. By no means am I religious or observant. But I do believe in God, and I do believe that we are not on this Earth by mere coincidence. I also believe that one can still be committed to science and empirical observation while not having to be an atheist or agnostic.

Rabbi Harold S. Kushner had us consider the role of God when life takes a dive and goes very wrong. He did this in his highly acclaimed book, *When Bad Things Happen To Good People* (1981). The rabbi suffered a major loss by the early tragic death of his own son from a rare genetic disease. The book was a result of the rabbi's attempt to make sense of his pain and to offer both personal and clerical wisdom to others. Kushner noted how people question their religious beliefs during periods of severe difficulty. One may live a moral and good life, yet still face major stressors and life changing events. Most people in these circumstances see themselves as *deserving* better. They are unable to fathom the *unfairness* of it all, and can easily turn against God, thus misplacing blame for their extremely unfortunate situations.

Kushner points out that God created the universe with all its wonders for humans to inhabit and share with other life forms. It came as a package with certain innate characteristics that define existence. It has some level of predictability, as seen by the general laws of physics and science. But randomness and probability are huge components of the universe, as well, and this is a fact that cannot be refuted. For example, there is no way of ever really knowing whether you are in the wrong place at any given time. Could you predict with 100% certainty where and when you will encounter a sudden life-threatening event? You could be sitting in a movie theater enjoying a film or just crossing the street when harm comes your way. The same is true when disease strikes. You just don't know. Despite your efforts at prevention, complete control of all circumstances is just not in your hands.

Control of what you do in this world, however, is another thing entirely. I emphasize what *you* do, not others. *Free will* or freedom of choice is a characteristic that cannot be overlooked. Humans have the ability to think for themselves and this often leads to positive things, such as important contributions to society and civilization. However, it is unfortunate that this freedom also leads to evil much too often, with pain and suffering as a result. Kushner tells us that these aspects of existence leave God out of the equation. God is not to be blamed for all misery, and cannot be responsible for individual actions and moral decisions.

What then is the purpose of prayer and religious faith? Kushner shares the notion that prayer and religion is a communal experience. To be part of and cared for by others is a spiritual need and it can be fulfilled through religious engagement. What brings us closer to others and also gives life more meaning is the ability to forgive and to love. Prayer to God for monetary wealth or a miraculous change of life events may only lead to more disappointment and even despair. According to Kushner, prayer may offer the strength and inspiration to better cope with difficult personal situations beyond the power seen or experienced anywhere else. It offers us comfort and support that nourishes the soul.

In the world of health and medical care, doctors are recognizing that religious beliefs, affiliation, and prayer may have more of a role than previously expected for patients undergoing surgical procedures and for those in process of healing (Davis, 2001). Religious people tend to cope better with stress, are more optimistic, and attribute more purpose and meaning to their suffering from long term disease, chronic pain, or the loss of a loved one. Prayer as a form of meditation leads to a calming of the human body, which helps individuals to better tolerate medical procedures and contributes to a speedier recovery.

Moreover, religious people who attend church, mosque or synagogue tend to live healthier lives. They spend less time in hospital care, are less likely to die from stroke or post cardiac surgery, and have a lower overall death rate from cardiovascular disease and cancer. In the mental health sphere, depression appears less frequently within the religious sector, and when it does occur, people get better faster.

There is also growing evidence that healing is accelerated when someone else prays for you, either individually or in a group. This prayer may be directly at your bedside or from a distance. Knowing that someone is praying for you may elicit a powerful healing effect within you. It affirms that you are not alone in trying to overcome your struggles. Although the jury is still out regarding this topic, it is surely worthy of further investigation.

In recent years, the evangelical Christian pastor Rick Warren demonstrated the power of community and "spiritual motivation" by inspiring his congregation at the Saddleback

Church in Lake Forest, California. Although his views are somewhat controversial, the mission of his church was to work together toward a goal of achieving a healthier lifestyle. They made a commitment to follow in the direction of "faith, food, fitness, focus, and friends," as outlined by their pastor in what was called *The Daniel Plan*, named after Daniel in the Bible (Warren, Amen, & Hyman, 2013). After a year of following this plan, the large congregation of this megachurch reportedly lost 250,000 pounds. There were also testimonials about individuals no longer having back pain, avoiding surgery and having "relief from dramatic mood swings" (Rochlin, 2013).

People can and do change with the help of spiritual and religious conviction. This is commonly known in the history of human experience. When there is a change in *collective consciousness*, a change emerges in the culture and institutions that are critical to our everyday lives. Spiritual and religious beliefs support a value system that is often reflected in our political and social views. These values become a part of our internal barometer and determine our sense of justice—what we consider to be our God-given rights, and what we regard as acceptable behavior in our society.

Religious leaders have taken responsibility in guiding us toward social change. For example, Martin Luther King, Jr., a Baptist minister who led the United States civil rights movement in the 1950's and 60's, had a dream of social change and justice. His life message and legacy continues to be just as important and relevant for now as it will be for the future. Pope Francis, the humble leader of the Roman Catholic Church at the time of this writing, was named *Time* magazine's 2013 Person of the Year. This recognition was for using his religious power to begin a change in the "tone and temperament" within the Vatican and the Church as a whole. This has been seen in his style of leadership and in the attitude taken toward the role of women in the church, gay relationships, divorce, contraception and abortion. While maintaining the traditional conservative policies, his position has been less judgmental, allowing for more tolerance and an evolving culture. Further, he has been proactive in dealing with the Church's sexual abuse scandal by creating a commission to help the victims of molestation by priests. He has been using the papacy to return the Church to its original values of caring for the poor and downtrodden (Chua-Eoan, & Dias, 2013; Gibbs, 2013).

Clergy frequently find themselves in a counselor role and are required to prepare for this in their academic studies. In years past, I had a client who struggled with self-proclaimed "unclean thoughts." He was deeply guilt-ridden and depressed. Being a religious and churchgoing man, his obsessive inclinations were getting the best of him. He was beginning to think of these thoughts as the gateway to hell. It was clear that he needed the right kind of reassurance, and it wasn't going to come from me. We both came to realize that this would be better achieved in the comforting hands of an understanding and qualified person from the clergy. While *pastoral counseling* is not necessary for everyone in this situation, he in particular believed that the only credentials he could trust were those accepted by his religious faith.

Another client who suffered for many years with schizophrenic illness thought differently about where he should turn for help. Despite the limitations of his illness, we were able to form a meaningful therapeutic relationship. One day he spontaneously expressed words of sincere appreciation. He gave unsolicited praise and referred to me as a "caring man doing God's work." It was a true blessing to remember and hold dear to my heart. To this day, his words resonate as he spoke about my efforts at helping with his recovery. Whether it is a person of cloth or a secular clinician, one cannot deny the importance of human connection in the process of healing.

To better understand and connect with clients, the modern

day mental health clinician is schooled in such areas as spiritual assessment and cultural diversity. These are competencies expected for practice in today's world and they are working their way into programs of graduate education. Psychiatric facilities nowadays are more actively using a chaplain as part of the therapeutic team for spiritual assessment and recommendations. If you are a patient within a health care setting, don't be shy about asking for chaplain services, if this is your desire.

Since *prayer* is an important part of spirituality and religion, it is only appropriate that I take this opportunity to share one that is commonly known and has been extremely helpful to many. During my years of clinical social work practice, I have always kept a copy of Reinhold Niebuhr's *Serenity Prayer* hanging close on the wall and in plain sight. I knew it to be a guiding principle of Alcoholics Anonymous (AA), but always considered it applicable to all other life problems. It reads as follows:

> *Grant me the serenity to accept the things I cannot change,*
> *The courage to change the things I can,*
> *And the wisdom to know the difference.*

These brilliant and powerful words, penned by a theologian, helped many of my clients over the years as they searched for solutions and strength to cope. The prayer also had special meaning to me, as I tackled many complicated issues over my career.

At this juncture, I want to give a personal account of experiences beyond my clinical work with clients. On three clear occasions I have personally felt something that I can hardly explain. These experiences took place during significant events in my life, two times when I was standing before the Torah at the synagogue that I barely attended, and another single time while viewing the Western Wall in Israel.

At the synagogue we were celebrating the bat and bar mitzvahs of my children. This is a rite of passage, a time when Jewish girls and boys are brought before the community as adults. The experience in Israel was during a pilgrimage visit. During all three situations I felt a wave of intense warmth throughout my body and a tingling rush of pressure up to my head and scalp. It was a strange but comforting feeling, a feeling of a presence with me that surrounded my being. Perhaps this feeling was pride for my children or reverence at standing in the midst of holiness. It could have been brought on by my own thoughts, telling myself how much in awe I felt. To this day, however, a part of me continues to wonder and to be *in* wonder about these moments. How can I make sense of them? What is the true interpretation? I was left with the belief that it is indeed possible for humans to have genuine spiritual experiences. It does not mean that you are crazy. Perhaps you are just very fortunate.

To promote the value of spirituality and religion even further, one might consider the age-old question of life after death. This might sound a bit hokey, and when thinking about the woman on television who calls herself a Medium, I too have a lot of difficulty taking it seriously. However, there are many seemingly legitimate accounts of people with near death experiences. One that is particularly striking comes from a person of science, a neurosurgeon who fell into a coma when afflicted by E. coli meningitis. Eben Alexander wrote a fascinating account of his near death experience as he fell deeper into what might be considered another time and place. His book, *Proof of Heaven* (2012), is an account of something he initially found hard to believe, and tried to make sense of by using his well versed scientific knowledge. Here, again, there is no clear explanation for what he experienced. After reading his true story as only he could tell it, the reader is left with a unique view of the soul, spirit and existence of a higher power in another realm. His vivid description seems to lessen the natural fear about the eventuality of death.

All religions have laws, customs, and rituals for periods of celebration and mourning. The structure is there for believers to have their faith comfort them as they adjust to major changes in their lives. We all look forward to joyful occasions to share with friends and loved ones. But, when sadness strikes, it is never welcome. When a loved one dies the bereaved are helped to respect the dead and express grief. There are various rules for funeral arrangements, dress, community, prayer, remembrance, and reintegration of one's own life. It is a time to consult the clergy who is there to support and guide you. For those of you who do have a religious affiliation and can achieve comfort in this way, I recommend that you do just that. Go ahead and call your priest, rabbi, pastor, or imam. It is helpful to recognize that grief and mourning are expected as part of a natural healing process. Of course, this process is also well known by all mental health professionals, and they too are available for consultation, if needed.

Understanding the role of spirituality and religion is consistent with the social work person-in-situation practice model. Spirituality and religion provide meaning to the lives of many individuals, and can be an important ingredient in the journey to better mental health.

22

Humor

Let's lighten up a bit! I want to talk about *humor* and laughter having an important role in everyday living and emotional health. A good laugh eases tension and improves relationship bonds. There are many health benefits with positive effects on blood pressure, respiration, and the body's immune system. Laughter helps reduce aches and pains, and it gives us respite from focusing on physical discomforts. When we are having fun, our spirits are lifted and this feels good. When feeling happy, we are not experiencing sadness, anger, or frustration at the same time. Looking at the humor in things can change our perspective and help us to become better problem solvers. We don't have to take ourselves so seriously or consider all bad situations as catastrophic events. With the inclusion of humor, life can become more bearable and manageable.

So, how many clinical social workers does it take to change a light bulb? Answer: Only one, but the light bulb must want to change. Of course, the social worker will also want to know more about the bulb, lamp, and lighting situation. Does the bulb have the correct wattage for the lamp? Does it provide the right amount of luminescence for the area? How is this area used? Is it for reading or some other task? What other changes, if any, would make the situation better? This humorous account playfully tells you something about what to expect when you see a clinical social worker as a therapist. Humor is a device used to entertain, but it is also an effective way to make a point, convey an important idea, or teach a lesson.

We are all aware of the comedians and satirical humorists who use keen observations of familiar behavior to rant about and mock social standards, politics, and cultural norms. George Carlin was a master of this with his heady unabashed approach. This type of humor is also seen in the standup routines of Jerry Seinfeld, all the late night talk show hosts and the self-deprecating work of Woody Allen. Unlike George Carlin, their shticks are cleaned up without embellishing four-letter words. The slapstick comedy of the Marx Brothers and the Three Stooges also made us chuckle as kids because of their ludicrous scripts and hysterical antics.

We laugh at both types of humor nowadays with the weekly broadcasts of *Saturday Night Live*. Situational comedies on television further entertain us by stretching reality and making light of various lifelike events. They match up different personalities sharing a realistic life conflict and use exaggerated responses by the characters to strengthen the plot and make it funny. *Curb Your Enthusiasm, Modern Family, Blackish*, and *The Middle* are all good examples of this. We can all identify with these characters in their fictional conundrum. However, when facing similar but real circumstances in our own lives, we don't necessarily find them so funny.

In the therapy session, humor has a place but it can also be obstructive and may not always be appropriate. For example, if you are a client repeatedly using jokes or funny stories in the session, your behavior may be interfering with your progress. This is known as *resistance*, merely a way of reducing intensity, and avoiding feelings of anxiety or unacceptable impulses. The therapist's role is to assess whether this is occurring and point it out, if necessary. A good therapist has good timing, is supportive, tactful and wants to help you move forward. An incongruent presentation by a client is often better dealt with at the time that it occurs. By pointing out this discrepancy, the client is made aware of the behavior and can acquire a better understanding of its dynamics. Learning how to genuinely feel and express oneself in a healthy way is one of the positive outcomes of the therapeutic experience.

A therapist may sometimes use humor to lighten things up and bond with the client. And sometimes humor is used to make a crucial point, teach a valuable lesson or offer an important insight. Clients who are fragile, especially those who enter therapy with shame-based problems, may not take well to this humor. They may feel ridiculed, insulted, or put down by the therapist. Clearly this is a situation when a well-intentioned tactic has failed. It is better to tell your therapist if you are feeling offended. A shift in the dialogue is expected and hopefully any damage to the therapeutic relationship can be repaired.

Albert Ellis advocated the use of humor and fun in psychotherapy to highlight the absurdities in life and especially in his clients' thinking. In *A Garland of Rational Songs* (1977), Ellis rewrote song lyrics to old popular classics, such as "The Band Played On," "Tea for Two," and "The Battle Hymn of the Republic." He created a collection of humorous songs to enjoy with his clients and he occasionally sung them in what he described as his "broken baritone" voice. They were encouraged to use REBT ideas to overcome their problems while having some fun as part of the process. The songs conveyed numerous messages, such as giving up laziness, working hard in therapy, and recognizing how procrastination, perfectionism, and faulty expectations interfere with life goals. Other topics included dealing with love, rejection, addiction, depression and anxiety. I'd like to share with you one of my favorites, which is clearly dated but still relevant. The version by Ellis is titled "I'm Just Wild About Worry," sung to the original tune of "I'm Just Wild About Harry," by Eubie Blake (1921):

Oh, I'm just wild about worry
And worry's wild about me!
We're quite a twosome to make life gruesome
And filled with anxiety!
Oh, worry's anguish I curry
And look for its guarantee!
Oh, I'm just wild about worry
And worry's wild about
Never mild about
Most beguiled about me!

Let me encourage you to work at writing your own song, using a familiar melody. If you're younger than me, then I'm sure you'll use a more modern tune. Whatever the choice of genre, it can be used as a reminder and a valuable tool to restructure your own irrational thoughts and disturbing emotions. Of course, it can also be a humorous and fun exercise toward the overall goal of improved mental health and wellness. If you decide to do this, don't forget to share your creativity with your therapist.

Whether the wisdom comes from your therapist, a friend, or a family member, it is clearly good advice to add humor and laughter to your life. In chapter 13, I spoke about the important elements of a stable marriage. If we were to take a survey today, I'd bet a huge number of lifelong partners would credit humor and laughter for keeping their relationships alive. When asked, they'd say, "We've stayed together all these years because my partner is a good person, treats me with respect, and makes me laugh."

Comic relief goes a long way to enrich and fortify a relationship. After forty-plus years of my own marriage, I can vouch for the value of humor on a regular basis. A good belly laugh always seems to work wonders. If you ask me, I'd prescribe a daily dose. So, ladies and gentlemen of my reading audience, here's what I want you to do at least once every day: LOL (laugh out loud)!

23

Some Final Words

Congratulations! If you got this far in the book, you've read about various topics intended to inform and prepare you for therapy. Hopefully some of this information was helpful to you and can be used to make your journey more productive. If anything was unclear, don't hesitate to ask your therapist about it.

Not everything will pertain to your particular situation so just refer to the chapters that you found most helpful and try to get the most out of them. You may need to reread these chapters, highlighting phrases and marking notes in the margins. Taking an active approach will help you to learn and having this knowledge is a good thing. It will help you to better understand the nature of your problems and the process of therapy.

Go ahead and thank yourself for getting this far. A lot was packed into these pages and I'm glad you made it through.

As a clinical social worker, I have recommended this profession for viewing the client as a whole person with clinical work focusing on the person-in-situation perspective. This is a more comprehensive approach than most other therapists use because of its attention to both the individual and environment. Biological, psychological, familial, social, political, economic, cultural and spiritual factors are all taken into account. Interventions then follow accordingly as a collaborative experience, building on strengths and available resources.

The job of a clinical social worker is not easy and the pay is not great. But the intangible rewards are enough to motivate some special people to enter and stay in this line of work. Our clients are also special people with unique qualities and interests. We truly believe they are good people who deserve to get better, just like you.

How are you now feeling? Did I do my job? Do you know more about what you are getting yourself into? Do you consider yourself more prepared for therapy and more able to fully participate? Are you ready?

If you've found the principles here helpful, you might want to turn your attention to WilliamLKnupp.com, the companion website to this book. There you will find workbook items, tasks, and forms for your active therapy. Use them by filling in the spaces and completing the exercises as appropriate. Print them out freely. Certainly ask your therapist for guidance with selecting those resources that would work best for you.

Try to move forward with an adventurous spirit and positive attitude. Be realistic in your expectations and hopeful about the future. Your journey will not be completed overnight but you'll eventually get there. You have my best wishes and full support! Be well!

References

Alexander, E. (2012). *Proof of heaven*. New York: Simon & Schuster, Inc.

American Psychiatric Association. (1994). *Diagnostic and statistical manual of mental disorders* (4th ed.). Washington, DC: American Psychiatric Association.

Bard, J.A. (1980). *Rational emotive therapy in practice*. Champaign: Research Press.

Beck, A.T. (1976). *Cognitive therapy and the emotional disorders*. New York: International Universities Press.

Beck, A.T., Rush, J.A., Shaw, B.F., & Emery, G. (1979). *Cognitive therapy of depression*. New York: The Guilford Press.

Beckfield, D.F. (2004). *Master your panic and take back your life!* (3rd ed.). Atascadero, CA: Impact Publishers.

Berne, E. (1964). *Games people play: The psychology of human relationships*. New York: Grove Press.

Bourne, E.J. (1995). *The Anxiety & Phobia Workbook* (rev. 2nd ed). Oakland, CA: New Harbinger Publications, Inc.

Bradshaw, J. (1988). *Healing the shame that binds you*. Deerfield Beach: Health Communications, Inc.

Brantley, J. (2007). *Calming your anxious mind* (2nd ed.). Oakland, CA: New Harbinger Publications, Inc.

Brown, R. (1965). *Social psychology*. New York: The Free Press.

Burns, D.D. (1980). *Feeling good: the new mood therapy*. New York: HarperCollins Publishers.

Chua-Eoan, H., & Dias, E. (2013). The people's pope. *Time*. Vol. 182. No. 26, 46-75.

Davis, J. L. (2001). *Can prayer heal?* WebMD. Retrieved from http://www.webmd.com/balance/features/can-prayer-heal.

Dryden, W., & DiGiuseppe, R. (1990). *A primer on rational emotive therapy*. Champaign: Research Press.

Ellis, A. (1962). *Reason and emotion in psychotherapy*. Secaucus: The Citadel Press.

Ellis, A. (1973). *Humanistic psychotherapy*. New York: McGraw-Hill Book Co.

Ellis, A. (1977). *A garland of rational songs*. New York: Institute for Rational Emotive Therapy.

Ellis, A., & Grieger, R. (1977). *Handbook of rational-emotive therapy*. New York: Springer Publishing Company, Inc.

Ellis. A., & Harper, R.A. (1978). *A new guide to rational living*. No. Hollywood: Wilshire Book Co.

Ellis, A. (1998). *How to stubbornly refuse to make yourself miserable about anything—yes, anything!* New York: Citadel Press.

Ellis, A. (2001). *Feeling better, getting better, staying better*. Atascadero: Impact.

Festinger, L. (1957). *A theory of cognitive dissonance*. New York: Row, Peterson.

Festinger, L. & Carlsmith, J.M. (1959). Cognitive consequences of forced compliance. *Journal of Abnormal and Social Psychology*, 58, 203-210.

Freud, S. (1961). Translated from German by Strachey, J. *Civilization and its discontents*. New York: W.W. Norton &

Company, Inc.

Gibbs, N. (2013). The choice. *Time*. Vol. 182. No. 26, 44-45.

Hafner, A. J. (1992). *Anger, discover your personal power to change*. Center City: Hazelden.

Harris, T.A. (1969). *I'm ok—you're ok*. New York: Harper & Row.

Hauck, P.A. (1973). *Overcoming depression*. Philadelphia: The Westminster Press.

Hauck, P.A. (1975). *Overcoming worry and fear*. Philadelphia: The Westminster Press.

Hersh, J.K. (2013). *The suicide detective*. The New York Times Magazine, Sun. July 14, pg 8.

Hyman, B.M., & Pedrick, C. (1999). *The OCD workbook*. Oakland: New Harbinger Publications.

Jacobson, E. (1962). *You must relax*. New York: McGraw Hill Book Company, Inc.

Jacobson, E. (1929, 1938 rev. ed.) *Progressive relaxation*. Chicago: University of Chicago Press.

Kabat-Zinn, J. (1994). *Wherever you go there you are*. New York: Hyperion.

Kabat-Zinn, J. (2013). *Full catastrophe living*. New York: Bantam Books.

Kushner, H. S., (1981). *When bad things happen to good people*. New York: Avon Books.

Ladouceur, R., & Lachance, S., (2007). *Overcoming pathological gambling: therapist guide*. New York: Oxford University Press.

Ladouceur, R., & Lachance, S., (2007). *Overcoming your pathological gambling: workbook*. New York: Oxford University Press.

Maultsby, M.C., & Hendricks, A., (1974). *You and your emotions*. Lexington: Rational Self Help Books.

Meichenbaum, D.H. (1972). Cognitive modification of test anxious college students. *Journal of Consulting and Clin-*

ical Psychology, vol. 39 (3), 370-380.

Meichenbaum, D. (1985). *Stress inoculation training.* New York: Pergamon Press.

Milgram, S. (1963). Behavioral study of obedience. *Journal of Abnormal and Social Psychology*, 67, 371-378.

Milgram, S. (1974). *Obedience to authority: an experimental view.* New York: Harper & Row, Publishers Inc.

National Association of Social Workers. (2013). *Mental health.* Retrieved from http://www.naswdc.org/pressroom/features/issue/mental.asp.

Nepo, M. (2000). *The book of awakening.* San Francisco: Conari Press.

Powell, T. (2000). *The mental health handbook.* Brackley, UK: Speechmark Publishing Ltd.

Reilly, P.M., Shopshire, M.S., Durazzo, T.C., & Campbell, T.A. (2002). *Anger management for substance abuse and mental health clients: participant workbook.* Pub No. (SMA) 02-3662. Rockville: U.S. Department of Health and Human Services.

Rochlin, M. (2013). The purpose driven diet. *Parade Magazine.* 12/1 issue, 9-14.

Segal, Z.V., Williams, J.M.G., & Teasdale, J.D. (2002). *Mindfulness-based cognitive therapy for depression: a new approach for preventing relapse.* New York: The Guilford Press.

Shiraldi, G.R. (2001). *The self-esteem workbook.* Oakland: New Harbinger Publications, Inc.

The Rabbinical Assembly. (1985). *Siddur Sim Shalom.* New York: The United Synagogue of America.

Walen, S.R, DiGiuseppe, R. & Wessler, R.L. (1980). *A practitioner's guide to rational-emotive therapy.* New York: Oxford.

Warren, R., Amen, D., & Hyman, B.M. (2013). *The Daniel Plan: 40 days to a healthier life.* Grand Rapids, MI: Zondervan.

Wessler, R.A., & Wessler, R.L. (1980). *The principles and practice of rational-emotive therapy.* San Francisco: Jossey-Bass Publishers.

World Health Organization. (2019, September 17). Depression. Retrieved from https://www.who.int/news-room/fact-sheets/detail/depression

Whitefield, C.L. (1987). *Healing the child within.* Deerfield Beach: Health Communications, Inc.

Index

Beck, A.T. xx, 118, 141
behavioral activation 119
belief system 33
Berne, E. 88
best practice xx, 4
bipolar disorder 95, 114, 133
Blake, E. 158
blame 44
Blarney Stone 108
Boreali, F. ii
Bradshaw, J. 88

C

can't-stand-it-itis 44
Carlin, G. 156
Carlsmith, J.M. 28
catastrophizing 41, 42
childhood trauma 85
Chua-Eoan, H. 151
claustrophobia 102
clinical social worker 4
codependency 73
cognitive behavioral therapy (CBT) xix, xx, 100, 104, 118
cognitive restructuring 98, 108
cognitive therapy xx, 119
cognitive triad 119
collective consciousness 150
commitment 71

communication 68
communication breakdown 69
compulsivity 93
computed tomography (CT) scan 142
confidentiality 6
consequences 48, 49
consequential thinking 97
coping statements 108
cortisol 104
culture 77

D

The Daily Record of Dysfunctional Thoughts 53
The Daniel Plan 150
Davis, J.L. 149
deep breathing 106
defense mechanisms 97
delusion 134
demand thoughts 39
denial 73
depression 113
depressive delusion 135
depressive neurosis 116
diagnosis 13, 19
Dias, E. 151
distorted thinking xx
dopamine 117, 137
dysthymia 116

E

ego 97
electroconvulsive therapy
  (ECT) 5
Ellis, A. xx, 37, 39, 44, 47,
  118, 141, 157
emotional wellness xviii
enabling 73
endogenous depression
  117
environmental therapy 10
ergophobia 102
exogenous depression 117
exposure and ritual prevention (ERP) 99

F

family therapy 10
fear 104
Festinger, L. 28
fight or flight reaction 104
free will 127, 148
Freud, S. 96

G

gender identity 76
generalized anxiety 36, 101
genotype 15
Gibbs, N. 151
Glick, B. i
glutamate 137
goodness of fit 7, 11

grandiose delusion 134
group therapy 10

H

hallucination 136
Harris, T.A. 88
Hauck, P. 104, 119
Hersh, J.K. 116
high blood pressure 121
high-risk situations 97
homework xix, 48, 52
humor 155
Hyman, B.M. 99, 150
hypoglycemia 117
hypothyroidism 20, 117

I

id 97
imagery 107
impulse control disorder
  95
impulsivity 93
individual therapy 9
infidelity 72
inner child 86, 88
inner circle 63
intentional inefficiency
  130
in vivo exposure 109
irrational beliefs 37, 49, 52

K

King, M.L. 150

133
schizophrenia 133
secondary anxiety 104
seething anger 131
Seinfeld, J. 156
self-acceptance 87
self-esteem 86, 87
self-indoctrination 32
self-instruction 108
self-monitoring 124
self-persuasion 108
self-praise 108
self-righteous anger 123
self-talk 35, 37
Serenity Prayer 152
serotonin 117, 137
sex 72
sexual orientation 76
shame 86, 87
Shiraldi, G.R. 86
social intervention 11
social work xx
somatic delusion 135
spirituality 147
splitting 76
stomach ulcer 121
stress inoculation training
    (SIT) 108
stroke 118
suicidal ideation 114
superego 97
sympathetic nervous system
    104
symptom 19

T

thought stopping 125
Three Stooges 156
timeout 125
Torah 152
toxic shame 88
transactional analysis 88
transference 97
traumatic brain injury
    (TBI) 142
treatment 19
trigger 102, 124

V

Valium 110
Vatican 150
vitamin B12 deficiency 117

W

Warren, R. 149, 150
Weight Watchers 34
Westbrook, A. ii
Western Wall 152
what if thinking 103, 108
WilliamLKnupp.com 53,
    106
workaholic 71

X

Xanax 110
xenophobia 102

Y

Z

www.ingramcontent.com/pod-product-compliance
Lightning Source LLC
Chambersburg PA
CBHW021504090426
42739CB00007B/462